Child Who Hates Her Father

And The Mother Who Caused It!

FORMER U.S. MARINE
CLELAND JAMES
FIGHTS A PERSONAL BATTLE
WITH PARENTAL ALIENATION SYNDROME
AND ESTRANGEMENT

The Child Who Hates Her Father

This book is being dedicated to all of the fathers out there who love and care about their child more than anything in the world, and have done everything they can for them, despite the government system that tears us away. There are too many fatherless children out there due to this and hopefully a loving father out there will know they are not alone. If a father really cares about their children, they become the most important person in their lives, beyond their wife.

I would also like to dedicate this book to my departed Grandmother Delila and departed Grandfather James.

I would also like to give credit to my 2 younger children James, and Michelle, who God Almighty sent to me to give me hope and love.

I would like to give further gratitude for my loving parents Bobby James and Linda James for raising me the right way, giving me the strength to carry on, picking me up when I fell, and guiding me through some of the worst times of my life, and my loving wife Mary who has personally walked through most of this with me and has stayed by my side through thick and thin.

Who Am I?

I grew up out in the country and went in the Marine Corps. I did police work, was a nationally registered EMT trained by the Navy, and periodically worked in conjunction with the FBI and DEA at Quantico, VA. I also had the responsibility of guarding the president of the United States when he was on base or the surrounding area, and working with the Secret Service. I additionally had alternate roles later in technology.

A parent unfortunately doesn't have a user's manual to raise a child, and sometimes we do things to protect and ensure the safety of our child just like many parents before us. Sometimes we are right, sometimes we are wrong; but it is done in the best interest of the ones we love.

Disclaimer: Everything that is written in this book is my personal observations, my experiences, and my opinions. If you read this book, you agree not to hold the writer, the

*** *I swore I was going to tell my story in the past, and I am making good on my word!* ***
...Cleland James

The Child Who Hates Her Father
© Copyright 2016 by Cleland James
ISBN: 9781520140865

Preface

How do I even start with telling you about this nightmare of mine? As much as I and my family have been through, it is a blur of my past 18 years of my life; and it is hard to believe that that time has went by so fast. What happened is jaw dropping, and it has felt to me like I have had a child get killed and taken away from me. It isn't something that a parent should have to deal with; after all we are supposed to pass away before our child right? Granted, my child didn't actually die; but in my heart, my mind and my soul, down to the last cell in my body that is how it feels. No one knows their pain better than themselves unless there is someone out there who has had the exact same thing happen to them.

Writing this book, thinking about all that has happened, is one of the hardest, most challenging, tear wrenching things I have ever done in my life. Even the challenges I faced in the Marine Corps couldn't compare to the stress my shoulders have carried throughout this war. I won't even sugar coat this, it wasn't a battle, it was an ongoing war which was to never be won, and I was mostly in offensive, planning and hope mode the whole time. Hope that somehow my beliefs, my experience, my knowledge, my ethics, and my character would reflect who my child was to become.

Let's face it, the system is corrupted, skewed, one sided and not just. I am not just talking about the court system; I am talking Human Services, Social Services, or whatever you want to call these people. It is a bunch of Social Workers who have nothing better to do with their time than to investigate men, and believe women, not the other way around. Justice is defined as, "just behavior or treatment" and is also the same as fairness, evenhandedness and objective. Is that what they call the treatment of men? Not in my experience!

I hope my words, my experience, and my proof show how little "rights" we really have to our children, how the system needs to accept that men, not just women, are just as capable of raising children as women are. It is equal, fair, and balanced. Is it ok for a child to be living in their mother's house, and never see their father? According to the system, it is perfectly acceptable. Is it ok for a child to live with their father full time and never see their mother? Not a chance in hell I say. Does that sound equal to you?

Table of Contents

Chapter 1 - The Start of the Nightmare

This nightmare started in 1997, when I came home from my duty station at Quantico Virginia. I was visiting my grandmother in Flatwoods, Kentucky, and I received a phone call from one of the girls whom I had gone to high school with asking me to come over and visit. So that is exactly what I did, I was going over and be polite. That was the evening that started the last 18 years' worth of misery. When I arrived both of them were sitting in the living room, and I believe that they were slightly tipsy, although I couldn't be sure.

That evening we went out, and the girl whom had called me, had a plan to set me up with her friend Josie who I did not know. What did not happen was, Josie sitting in the front seat of my car, but rather Leslie who made herself comfortable in the passenger seat up front. With that scenario in place, I ended up speaking with Leslie more than Josie; and I really wasn't attracted to Josie to begin with. I had remembered going to school with Leslie, and I also had remembered Josie, both of them which were acquaintances at best in high school. Both of them were in JROTC, and so was I. The Marine Corps Junior ROTC was probably one of the best things that I had ever attended while I was in high school, and had set the stage for me going in the Marine Corps. As a matter of fact, at the time I entered into high school, I had previously left the middle school where I attended, and played second seat trumpet. I thought I was pretty good at playing that instrument, and wanted to carry it all the way through high school. What happened was that the marching band instructor, Mr. Thompson, at Greenup County High School, told me that I had to make a choice between the band and JROTC. I ended up turning my instrument in for the latter.

I can't remember exactly what we did while we were out, but I do remember driving around a lot. Once the evening was over, I ended up taking Josie home and Leslie remained in the vehicle. That is pretty much all that I remember of that night other than the fact that Leslie's attempt to set me up with her friend had failed. I do remember that my heart rate was up, I was sweating, and I was somehow falling for Leslie. She really was a pretty girl, and seemed nice, fun and appealing to me. This led to more talking, more visiting, and dating her.

Over the course of the next several months, while I was stationed at Quantico, Virginia, I would drive home every other weekend, on my 72 hour Liberty to see Leslie. It was an exhausting trip, as it took 8 hours to get to Kentucky, 8 hours to get back to the base, and less than 24 hours to visit Leslie. At the time Leslie was living in a trailer with her mother, father, and brother on the top of a ridge called, way back up on the top of a hill. If you have ever heard the expression, "the boonies", that is where she lived, in a broken down single-wide trailer. I never did judge her, or her family. I would sneak into the trailer in the middle of the night, so I wouldn't wake everybody in the house up, go back and crawl in bed with Leslie and knock out hard. After 8 hours in the vehicle you can imagine how tired I was. This went on for several months. One trip back from visiting Leslie, I was on the interstate heading back to base, and it was sprinkling rain. I was in the left passing lane of the interstate, traveling around seventy MPH, and there was a tractor-trailer in the right lane. I was passing the semi, and the next thing I know, he swerves over into my lane and causes me to steer left away from him.

The next thing I know, my driver's side front tire catches a wet patch of grass in the median from the rain, and pulls me right into the U shaped open median. My Dodge Neon that I was driving at the time started to fish-tail, left, then right, then left again. I was doing my best to hold the car from flipping, and hoping that I could get it to stop. I was completely wrong in my attempts. The next thing that happened should have killed me, but somehow didn't. My car caught a dry patch of grass, or dug down far enough in the dirt to get traction and my car came out of the median on the wrong side of the interstate, ramping out of the median, in the air over the highway and hit the hill head on at 70 MPH. How it didn't kill me, I don't know; but I do remember kicking the passenger door open and rolling down the hill on my face, cursing the semi, as if he could actually hear me. Not only was I terrified, shook up, the soreness hasn't even had the time to set in yet. What really was worrying me was that I was supposed to be back on duty the following morning approximately 8 hours from that time. There is a rule that you are not supposed to go outside of a certain mile range on your liberty time, which is your days off; but I was slightly bending the rules to see Leslie. I can't remember the intimate details of how I managed to get a bus ticket back to base, but I ended up getting back and spent the morning at the Navy Medical Clinic on base getting patched up.

During the course of all of this while I was on base, I was living in the Security Battalion Barracks, MCB Quantico, VA, with another Marine, who I shared the barracks room with, and had also worked with me at the Provost Marshal's Office. Let's just say that the living quarters were quite comfortable, compact, and unique. Since we worked opposite shifts, the TV was on frequently, and I didn't get much sleep. Two or three days out of the week after duty of 12 - 17 hours, we would get together in the platoon and do physical training consisting of a three mile run pushups pull-ups and whatever else that they had to train us on. Sleep was not in the regiment of training.

Chapter 2 - My Pregnant Wife

Sometime along the way, around September of 1997, Leslie got pregnant and we were trying to figure out a way to tell her mom and dad. At the time her father John, was working in a garage in South Shore, Kentucky, and doing general mechanics work for a garage there. I went down to give John a hand and spent all day working on brake jobs for a vehicle that he was working on. It was then that I had told John that Leslie was pregnant, and that she and I needed to get married. I really had grown to love Leslie and thought the world of her.

It was then that I had brought the news to my family, and we had begun to plan the wedding. Leslie had an idea to get Trudy Collins, a friend of her family involved in order to plan the wedding. I can't remember if Leslie was at Trudy Collins's house that day or not, but I clearly remember Trudy Collins telling me not to marry Leslie, that she was too wild, and not to be trusted. I don't know if Trudy Collins knew something that I didn't know at the time, or if she was just warning me about how Leslie was. It was only several years later that I found out some things that I will go into later. It is amazing how love will make you blind to warning. There could be a hurricane blowing in your face, and you would completely ignore it and walk right into it for someone you truly love. That is exactly what I did.

Leslie and I got our marriage license and ended up getting married. The wedding ceremony was performed at a "wedding chapel", in Greenup, Kentucky. It wasn't a church, but a business in the little mall area where there was an ordained minister who did this as a service to the community for a small fee. It was a small and quaint wedding where immediate family from both sides of the family had attended. It was short, sweet, and did the job. I had heard many years later that he was not truly licensed to do the ceremonies, so honestly I don't know if I was ever truly married or not. I can tell you this, maybe it's true, or not, but the wedding chapel didn't stay in business too long.

At this point, Leslie and I both moved to Quantico, Virginia, base housing, and started living our lives while I was still on active duty Marine Corps serving as a military police officer on base.

Leslie was not accustomed to living in a city environment, nor was she accustomed to having people around of a military nature. She had seemed to adjust quite well; however, I know that she was alone at home by herself quite a bit, long hours while I was on duty working. There were many days and nights, depending on my schedule, where I was gone anywhere between 12 and 17 hours on duty. I didn't understand then what I know now, and that is that a 17 year old girl needs family around, to talk with or spend time with. I understand now that it was very difficult on her to be alone by herself on a strange base with no one around to talk to. One of the hardest jobs I have heard in the Marine Corps is being a Marine's wife.

Some weeks later, arguments started to occur, causing problems between my wife and I, and making my job much more difficult to perform. I really did enjoy having her on base at the time, and I started to introduce her to several of the Marines wives that I knew. I would get her involved in some of our platoon outings, cookouts, and social gatherings. I took her to the base gym, where we would walk in the track, play basketball, lift weights, play racquetball, and do several of the other activities that they had at the Recreation Center. For the Marines and the Marines wives, and dependents', it was a handy way to keep in shape. I even took her to the Marine Corps Ball in 1998, where we were in formal dress and were able to mingle with the higher ranking officers and enlisted personnel. If you have never been to a Marine Corps Ball, it is a memorable occasion.

Chapter 3 - The Birth of My Amazing Daughter

On June 26th of 1998, my daughter was born. We had discussed several names to give her, as most parents do, and we had considered the name to give her. We spent several hours at the hospital when my wife was in labor, and the doctor gave her a spinal tap to relieve the pain. There were several nurses and staff in the delivery room with us, and I assisted with delivery of my child. The pain had caused severe upset stomach with my wife, and she practically projectile vomited on me. It missed me by a matter of inches. I just simply ignored it and kept on working. It was one of the longest, drawn out, and stressful times of my life. Waiting, monitoring, checking, talking, and more waiting was the extent of my day.

About an hour later my daughter was born, and it was one of the most remarkable, unique, and amazing experiences of my life. I immediately fell in love with my child, and took her over to the table to weigh her. She was a healthy eight pounds four and a quarter ounces. To this day, that was one of the most vivid, memorable moments of my life seeing my beautiful new daughter for the first time. She was absolutely beautiful with blue eyes, short and barely any blonde hair, and a look just like every new baby, confusion. That type of confusion as to where am I, who are you, and what am I doing here, and for that matter who am I? Although it's concerning, it is the one of the cutest things which that a parent like me could imagine seeing on her little precious face.

I can still feel the rush of blood going through my body today, even though it's been 18 years ago. The nurses and I put my cute little one on a roller bed, and started out the door, to take her to the nursery where all of the appropriate paperwork could be drawn up on our newly acquired child. Leslie grabbed my arm on the way out the door, and told me that she wanted her first name to be Kelsey. It was contrary to what she and I had discussed, but I nodded my head and took off down the hall.

What she didn't tell me was that, she wanted me to replace her name, not add on to her name. Long story short, my daughter ended up with four names which wasn't my wife's plan; but she had other things on her mind at this time, considering she just gave birth, and she was in extraordinary pain. Kelsey Brooke Morgan James, my first child, and the light of my life. If you're a parent, you can imagine the thrill of seeing this for the first time. Of course you walk by people out on the street who have children or have friends with children, pushing them around in strollers; but it's just not the same as having your own. It's just like when friends hand you their baby. Yes, they are fun to look at, fun to hold, fun to make funny faces at, and laugh with, but in the end you can simply hand them back to their parent and go about your merry way. Things really change when you're the one responsible for the child. You have to be the one to provide for them, to make sure there is food for them to eat, to make sure you bathe them, to change their nasty diapers, and to play with them. It is a 24-7 job, not a five minute meet-n-greet, if you understand what I mean!

All I can tell you was that we were ready for our child. Our apartment on base already had her crib, blankets, curtains, drawers, among the other things that we needed for our child. We decided that we were going to be prepared to get Kelsey all taken care of. Just like any new parent, started the sleepless nights, worrying about our child sleeping, and hours of going in there too admire the peaceful and tranquil look on her face. My worst fear was Kelsey would stop breathing in the middle of the night. You see in the news all the time of sudden infant death syndrome where exactly that happens, so it became an immediate fear of mine. Losing my child would tear my world in two, and I wasn't about to let that happen. I would rather post a guard in her room monitoring her all night before I would let that happen. Words cannot even explain the love that a father feels for his baby. This love, the feeling in your heart never ceases, and only gets stronger the longer your child is alive. To hold my baby, to gaze into her eyes, to cradle her in my arms, to kiss her, rock her to sleep and watch the little thing grow, is the most amazing thing. I know that I am not the only father who feels this way. Society and the culture think it's strange, and odd for a father to feel this way. Let me be the first to tell you, if it hasn't dawned on you or anyone else, it's not odd, and it's not strange. It is absolutely, one-hundred percent natural, and anyone who tells you different is a moron. I hate to be direct about this, but I am a father who has always felt this way, and it will never change. Yes, I am a one-hundred percent man, but I have a loving sensitive caring side to me as well, for anyone who truly knows me, will tell you.

I remember the challenges clearly as if it were yesterday. My poor little daughter would be in her room screaming at the top of her lungs, and me as a new young father not having the slightest clue what to do to soothe her, or calm her down. I have to be honest, I was confused and stressed and felt like I couldn't do anything. Now that I look back, I think she was lonely and wanted mommy and daddy to hold her is what it boiled down to, but we were trying our best to get her to sleep in her own bed. She really had one of the most ear piercing screams that could shatter glass. I didn't know until later in life that girls naturally have the ability to break glass with their shriek, but me being young, I didn't have a clue except this paranormal activity was happening to me frequently. I remember trying to drive in town, on the interstate, and on base with her screaming like that. It really puts a damper on concentration and I honestly don't know how I didn't wreck, but thanks to God I didn't. Let me put it to all new fathers this way, be prepared, if you have fine China, trade it in for something made of thicker glass, get a pair of earplugs for those times that you are ready to pull your hair out, and hold on tight, because it will be a long bumpy ride. I realize that you are probably laughing, for those fathers who have been through this know, and those who don't have a daughter yet, all I can tell you is just wait and you will understand why everyone who has daughters are laughing.

Leslie missed her family, so we took many trips back and forth between Virginia and Kentucky, taking our beloved daughter with us. One particular trip her friend Priscilla was at her grandmother's across the road visiting when we came in. For some reason, I thought it was a good idea to introduce her to another friend of mine who was also in JROTC with me at Greenup County High School. Those two started dating, and shortly got married as well. My friend was a year ahead of me in school and went in the Army at the end of my junior year. What I didn't know was that he was stationed about twenty minutes north of me at Ft. Belvoir Virginia. I remember sitting on duty at the fire station, where I was performing the duty of fire dispatch, along with another Marine who was military police on base at the time. It was mid-day, and I get this anonymous call from someone, and he said, you better know who this is. I was stunned, because it could have been anyone from the President of the United States down to the Colonel of Security Battalion. He told me who it was of which I replied, "Where in the heck are you?" He informed me of his location, and I was shocked since he was right up the road. What are the chances in that ever happening in the military - little to none? During this time, Priscilla moved to Ft. Belvoir base housing with her new husband since they were now married. Leslie and I made frequent trips to the base to visit since they were friends of ours.

I used to go to the Research and Development command at Quantico on a frequent basis to look things up on the internet, since they had an entire lab of computers setup for use of military personnel. I got tired of making these trips to the RDC so I decided that I was going to buy myself a laptop. It was a huge mistake, because Leslie didn't want me having one, and she had other plans for the money I had saved for things which "we needed more". I got dial-up internet since we already had a phone at the base housing. Keep in mind that this was 1998, and technology still had not taken off yet. The only real internet was that which the military used across the United States and International for sharing of files, but it was starting to become a more popular way of communication for the civilian sector. I used it to write emails, get online and chat, and some other things. One particular day when Leslie and I made one of our trips to our friends at the Army base, I decided that it was a good idea to take the laptop with me, of course I wanted to show my friend something that I had acquired on CD, which honestly, I shouldn't have been stupid enough to bring with me. Priscilla and Leslie were in the kitchen at the time, and her husband and I were in the bedroom. I was showing him what I had on disk, and Leslie walked in. She picked up the laptop, and smashed it on the hard tile floor in the bedroom, jealous and mad. Honestly I can't blame her for being mad, but that was a $1500 dollar laptop at the time, of which I didn't buy insurance on it, and she destroyed it in two seconds flat. I learned a hard lesson about not buying insurance. The screen was busted; the frame was broken in two, the keyboard keys missing or broken off. It was a complete and total wreck, of which now, we couldn't get our money back. It was gone and that was it. I could understand mad, but what I couldn't grasp, was the carelessness in destroying a two week old laptop.

Now sometime during this time, Leslie and I decided to approach the Navy Medical Hospital in Bethesda MD, to get some medical work done for her. About the time Leslie was 13 years old, before I ever met her, she and her mother were driving, Leslie in the passenger seat, and they were hit head on by a drunk driver. As a result of the accident, Leslie had a piece of the oncoming vehicle's headlight pierce her eye and blind her, which resulted in a complete loss of eyesight. Because of this, her doctor at the time, had created her a glass eye, painted to mimic the look of an actual eye, although you could tell it wasn't real, it served its purpose. Since it was several years later, Leslie needed to have another replacement glass eye made, and we went on several trips to Maryland. It took approximately 3 weeks, and detail to get the product made. She would sit and the artist, who was working on the drawing of her eye detail, would sit for hours with a paintbrush, colors and work carefully with his artistic strokes. After he was done, the eye cap was polished to a high luster and clear coat applied to keep it from dulling. This replacement was much better than its previous one, and lasted much longer.

Chapter 4 - Out of Hand

About the time that dear Kelsey was about 6 months old, things really started to really get out of hand. I am not sure what the real underlying problem was with my wife, but I can certainly tell you that it made life for me difficult to impossible. With my insane work schedule, my required continued training, physical fitness, keeping my apartment inspection ready at any moment, and vehicle maintenance, along with taking care of Kelsey, my relationship with Leslie started taking a bad road. Imagine being up all night, arguing with your spouse, and then trying to go to work? For those of you who have been through this, you know exactly what I am talking about. Most of the arguments were over useless, ridiculous stuff that should never call for a discussion, alone an argument. Again, at the time, I was 19 and she was 17, so imagine the young stupid arguments and conversations that we had. It wasn't all over adult issues, but rather mostly over childish nonsense. I am not saying that I was always right here, but a majority of the time, I had reason for putting my two cents out there on the table.

I remember at the time that I was working day shift, and I came home from work one evening from the police department on base and greeted by my wife. She brandished a 12-inch butcher knife from the kitchen, and backed me into the corner of the living room. I still had on my black gear, badge and was still in uniform. Just like a standard operating procedure with the Marine Corps, I left my pistol in the armory at the Provost Marshal's office. Leslie had accused me of cheating on her, because of my long work hours, and procedural requirements with the Marine Corps. I ended up picking up my Japanese katana sword, and unshielded it from the scabbard, threw the scabbard on the ironing board, and held it up like a dull butter knife, asking her to please put down the knife. Additionally, I picked up the portable phone and called the desk sergeant who relieved my shift, and informed him that my wife had a knife on me, threatening to kill me, which is exactly what she said. Sergeant Santos, who was the relieving desk sergeant and whom heard most of the conversation, sent all available police units to my apartment residence. Since it was a fellow Military Police officer, he took the issue very seriously. I didn't realize how seriously until several minutes later.

My wife, Leslie, got startled by the police sirens, and ran upstairs. She then grabbed my daughter of 6 months old, ran down the stairs and out the front door trying to evade the police officers. The military police officers stopped her on the sidewalk outside of the residence and detained her for questioning. At this point, I was still in my living room, phone in hand, sword on the couch, standing in awe, watching her run out the door. One of the Lance Corporals, military police, whom I worked with on opposite shift, asked me what had transpired and where the weapon was. I clearly explained to him that I had just got home from the police department, where he relieved me and told him about what just happened, and explained to him that my wife had the butcher knife downstairs but did not have the butcher knife when she came back down the stairs, after retrieving my daughter. I told him to go ahead and come upstairs with me, and we located the butcher knife in my daughter's bedroom closet covered by blankets where she was trying to hide the knife. With the Lance Corporal beside me, I reached into the closet and was able to locate the weapon and handed it to him. After this, he and I walked outside and I was in shock. There were 7 police units outside with lights on, and one of the fire trucks from the on base fire station that I worked with from time to time. I thought it was hilarious, because it was practically every police cruiser that we had from the police station, along with every police officer that I worked with on opposite shift and several firefighters that I knew as well. The neighborhood looked like a light show, and I started laughing. A police report was drawn up which I was responsible for writing, and it was signed off on by the on duty police officer. I ended up writing most of the report, since I was a trusted, cleared Military Police officer.

My company's 1st Sergeant, First Sergeant Larry King, not to be confused with the famous talk show host, ordered me to stay at the security battalion barracks for my own safety, until the situation could calm down and give us both ample time to relax. At that point, I had another military police officer go with me to my residence so that I could gather my belongings, my uniform, and other needed things such as hygiene. I moved into the security battalion barracks that night with another Marine who was my roommate, because that was my orders. This went on for several weeks, and I was not authorized to go to my own apartment, nor be around my own wife. It was difficult, since I couldn't see my own daughter either, and that alone was hard since she was my little baby.

Now since I couldn't go home, on my off duty time, and spend time with my wife and child, like I really wanted to do, I ended up going out to Weapons Training Battalion to visit another Marine whom I got to know really well. We went to combat training together prior to being stationed on Base, at Camp Lejeune North Carolina. We spent restless nights together, freezing our butts off, being lost in the woods, and starving together while in training. We went out on our weekend liberties together in town, and learned how to survive on our own. So once we got to Quantico, I was shocked to learn that Chris was there as well. He was really a good guy, and did what he could to accommodate me. We would get together and go out to eat in town, hit the malls, and go to the clubs to have a few drinks and get our minds off of what was going on. We were Marines, and that is what Marines do best besides fight.

One particular day, while I was still required to stay at the barracks, Chris was over at the barracks with me, and I think we were out back, or downstairs doing our laundry or something. I really can't remember what was going on at the time, but I do remember the duty NCO (Non-Commissioned Officer) finding me and telling me that my wife just walked in, went to my barracks room, and walked out. I was confused at this, since first off, she was not supposed to be at the barracks, second, it was the Military Police barracks where every single base police officer lives who is single, and lastly, because she had made herself so well-known because of all of the trouble, that she was well identified. I walked back to my assigned barracks room and behold, I see a condom and a nasty gram taped to my door. I shrugged, and went about my business at that point. Chris and I decided that we were going to drive out in town, just to get off the base for a little while. Since my wife had the car at the apartment, Chris and I took his mid-1990's Ford Mustang. On the way out the front gate of Quantico, we noticed that my ex-wife and Priscilla were following us. Chris was driving from what I remember, and I simply told him to lose them. Being a Mustang, Chris floored it and was rolling down route 1 well beyond the speed limit. I hunkered down in the passenger seat to make myself invisible, but what was the point? Again I was young and it was obvious that they knew I was in the vehicle. The next thing I knew, Chris bottomed out the car, and I asked what had happened. He ran over the hill down through the Allstate Insurance parking lot. At least we didn't have an accident, but that was one rough landing. I don't remember if they actually caught up with us or not, but we did the best we could do to evade them, since my orders clearly stated I was to not have contact with her. I didn't want to do that, but orders were orders and any veteran will agree with me that you do not want to disobey orders.

Chapter 5 - The Return

After about two months of separation, and all of the stress that went along with it, on top of my job with the military police office, my First Sergeant agreed to allow me to return to my on base housing apartment, so that I could continue my life with my wife and my child. It was a long and frustrating time away, and I was eager and excited to return to my own apartment away from the military barracks. I liked being able to have my own privacy, my own backyard, my own grill, and a place where I can park my own car. I even enjoyed the ability to drive my own vehicle. Even along with knowing about the problems that my wife Leslie and I were going through, it was nice to be home, to spend time with her and spend time with my daughter Kelsey. Sometime in the following weeks or months, Leslie, Kelsey, and I took a trip to Kings Dominion, of Richmond, Virginia about an hour and a half south of Base. I enjoyed being able to get out and take somewhat of a vacation away from base with my family. We spent the day there playing games walking around, pushing Kelsey in her stroller, and just enjoying the summer. We had a picture made that year at Kings Dominion which I still have somewhere. You should have seen how proud I was, standing beside my wife and my beautiful baby girl, who I loved more than anything in the world.

Not too long following that, there was another incident that took place on base, again, in my base housing apartment. I don't remember exactly what the argument was about, probably something stupid again, but I remember that it was in the bedroom, and Leslie got mad and ripped my shirt off my back, jumped on top of me and started hitting me in the back, scratching me on my back, and cursing me to no end.

4. That the Respondent is not stable and has been treated for mental problems at Snowden Hospital at Fredericksburg, Virginia in 1998 for attempted suicide and other emotional mental instabilities. That she has attempted suicide by taking pills and has tried to stab herself with a knife on another occasion and she has held a knife to her chest screaming, "I don't want to live anymore."

I tried to get away and went out in the hall. The next thing I know Leslie grabs me and throws me down the stairs. I tumbled the whole way down an entire flight of stairs. I can't remember exactly how I went about filing the report this time, but I do remember specifically having one of our Criminal Investigation Division NCOs take a picture of my back for record. Again First Sergeant King, who was simply trying to do the best he could for me, put me back in the security battalion barracks. This time, he ordered me and my wife to attend marriage counseling, through the Navy medical clinic, to resolve our issues. We attended marriage counseling for several weeks, however, my wife Leslie and I could not see eye to eye on a lot of things. The things that I had thought were obvious, and had easy resolutions we're not so obvious to my wife and we disagreed. What can I say, I tried to be reasonable; and I certainly tried the marriage counseling because I believed that there was a way for me and my wife to come to a resolution, or at least an understanding of how we should interact with one another to alleviate some of the tension in our family. I wanted to be married, and did everything that I possibly could to remain that way. It was and never had been my intention to solely marry Leslie because she was pregnant.

Not too long after the previous events, Leslie must have been having an extreme time coping with her problems. She blamed most of it on me, but usually those who have problems, not just my wife, will point the finger at someone else blaming them for their shortcomings, or their actions. It isn't just me, it's a proven fact that psychologically, that is what happens, and sometimes those people turn to drugs or alcohol to solve their problems, or so they think. One day, I had a long drawn out day on the road patrolling the base, again after 17 hours' worth of fun and excitement; I make it back to my base apartment, Kelsey only a baby of months old. I came in the front door of the apartment and no-one was in the living room, and no-one in the kitchen, so I figured they must be taking a bath. I walked upstairs and Kelsey was in her crib asleep, and Leslie was in our bed. Beside her was a huge bottle of acetaminophen (pain reliever), and she had taken pretty much all of them in the bottle. Keep in mind that at the time, not only was I a Police officer on base, but I was a certified EMT. I checked her pulse, it was weak. I checked her blood refill time and it was much slower than normal. She was pale, cold and clammy, and reflexes delayed. She was lethargic in her speech and was slurring. She was not on this earth at the time. I called the base Provost Marshal's office again and declared a medical emergency, told them to get our fire department and a medic squad out to my apartment pronto. They rushed her to the local hospital, where she was admitted into care for a couple of days for observation. They ended up pumping her stomach and putting her on intravenous fluids to flush out the excess chemicals in her blood. Luckily enough, she survived, but that was a seriously close call on her part for attempting to kill herself, and for what - attention? She was reaching out for some type of help, but bad attention is not good attention. Any type of delay on my part, coming home from work, and she would have been dead – without a shadow of doubt in my mind.

Chapter 6 – Rape or SmokeScreen?

Not too long after I was ordered again to go to security battalion barracks, I was at work at the Provost Marshal's office, standing outside getting some air and drinking some coffee. The same Criminal Investigation Division (CID) NCO, who took the pictures of my back named Brian, asked me if he could speak to me for a moment. We were friends and we were also colleagues, so I accommodated his request, as he was talking to me in official capacity, not as a chitchat session. He asked me if I knew about anything really recent in regards to my wife. I chuckled, and told him that First Sergeant King had put me at the barracks again, because of the incident which I had him take pictures of. He said that he wasn't aware of that, as he hadn't spoken to the First Sergeant, but he was married and lived in off base housing so he didn't hang around the barracks much to get word of what was happening around the base. He said, "Well, I don't know how to tell you this, so I am just going to come right out with it. Your wife filed a report of rape against a Marine at Weapons Training Battalion.", which was right out at the same place which my friend Chris was living. Brian never told me whom she filed the report against, nor did I ask as I was just under way too much pressure already. Honestly, at the time he asked me if I knew about this, I about passed out right where I stood. I knew that my wife and I had really gone through some rough times, but I was thinking to myself, why on earth would she want to draw that much attention to herself? I couldn't come up with any plausible excuse, nor could I think of any reason why this would occur - at the time!

A few weeks passed, and again I was back living in my on base apartment, with my wife and daughter. I never brought up to Leslie that I knew about the rape charge she had filed against the Marine at Weapons Training Battalion, and I never thought about asking Chris if he knew anything about it at the time. In 2016, I did ask him, and he didn't know anything about it, but I am sure if he did, he would have told me, because we are old friends and Marines. You know as well as I do, hindsight is always 20/20, and you could think of a million things that you would do different if you was to go back in time and get a redo, but we unfortunately can't turn back time, at least not yet in our technical stage of evolution. Not very long after this, I was again informed, by Brian, that my wife had come back in and dropped the rape charge that she had previously filed. I thought to myself, hmm, now if that rape really occurred why would my own wife, whom I already was stressed to no end over, would do something like that, turn around and file a charge against the Marine, then drop it. It didn't make any sense to me then and it sure as fire doesn't make any sense to me now. Would it make any sense to you? Maybe, being an outsider, looking in on my story - most likely you would.

I was inside of the looking glass, not standing outside looking in at the time. Had I been where I am today looking back, or where you are now looking at the story I am painting to you, I would have seen it. It was clear as day! My young wife, alone for hours on end, on a Marine Corps base, 8 hours away from any of her family, me at work 12-17 hours on rotating schedule. Maybe it was, and maybe it wasn't, but what I could tell you is that was sure strange that this incident even happened. All of the time we were fighting, all of the time that my wife was accusing me of cheating on her "multiple times", she had been the one sleeping around, and for that matter, at my own darn apartment. Would that get you mad, because I feel the anger in that? As God Almighty is my witness, I never cheated on her not one single time, and frankly I didn't want to or feel the urge to either.

Chapter 7 - Don't Do It!

This whole incident put a doubt in my mind, as to the validity, the certainty of my marriage with Leslie. I still forgave in my mind, but I never forgot what she had done. I carried on with everyday life, working hours on end with my position, and coming home to take care of my daughter. Sometime in the summer months, with my replacement vehicle, a Dodge Intrepid, I was having problems with my engine overheating. I didn't know anything about vehicle maintenance, as my father refused to teach me anything. He always told me, "Son, I want you to get educated, get a high paying career and pay someone else to do this type of work for you.", and I understood where he came from, so I dropped the idea about him teaching me mechanics, and went about my way. What is coming up was a life lesson for me. Never never never, if you don't know what you're doing with vehicles, try to flush your radiator. For that matter, don't even try to change your oil, put air in the tires, or check your brake fluid. Let someone qualified, and who has detailed knowledge on the subject do it. The other lesson I learned here is simply to "ask", before doing.

I went outside to my car, sometime on the weekend, and opened the hood of my car. Somehow in my mind, I thought I knew what I was doing, or could at least figure it out. Let me tell you how wrong I was right now. Me being the clean Marine I was, being taught how to clean anything spotless, I could at least figure out how to "flush" my radiator, right? Not a chance! I went in the apartment, and got the dawn dishwashing liquid, and dragged out the garden hose. I drained all of the radiator fluid out of the block into a bucket, and squirted in half a bottle of dawn, then topped off the radiator with water, and took it out for a spin to get the water hot, circulated through the motor, in hopes that I would clean and flush the proverbial crud out of the radiator and the engine to make it squeaky clean. By the time I got back, it looked like a sudsy mess all over the engine, dripping suds out from under the car, and a trail of breadcrumbs leading up to my parking spot where I had just pulled in. I called my dad panicked because of the results and he couldn't believe what I was telling him. He said something to the effect of, "Son, are you really that stupid.", and told me where I went wrong, and the first thing was I should have called him, and the second that there was flush that you get from the auto parts store. Even to this day, looking back, I felt like a complete idiot for thinking that was ok. I am lucky that I didn't destroy my mode of transportation. I drained all of the crud, suds, and water out of the engine again, and kept running water through there, until it was all cleaned out. All that was ever wrong with the overheating issue was that I didn't have enough of the correct type of fluid in the overflow tank. What did I know, I was still a kid.

After this was over, there was a slight leak in the radiator. Apparently I had flushed it to the point that it broke loose crud holding the radiator together on the inside. The walls of the radiator must have already been thin, or that wouldn't have happened, but I remember coming out to the car on multiple other occasions later and seeing small puddles of green fluid from the car. I was thinking that I should replace the part itself, but the leak wasn't really that bad, so I just let it go for the time being.

Chapter 8 - An Accident

Not very long after the crazy incident with my Dodge Intrepid came a worrisome event that I thought had done permanent damage to my little darling of a baby girl Kelsey. Our on base apartment had old government standard tile, and wooden staircases leading upstairs. I was taking Kelsey upstairs and I slipped and dropped the poor little thing, like a lead weight, right on the stairs, and at the same time, I fell on my face and slid a few feet back. She hit the stairs so hard that she buckled up. My heart sank into my feet. You know that sick feeling that comes over you, when you think you just did something that you can't take back, or that someone died? Yes, that is the feeling that hit me. I was speechless, frightened, and immediately sick to my stomach. I called 911, spoke to the Desk Sergeant at the Military Police office, and told him to get an ambulance to my house pronto. He sent a police unit, the fire team, and the ambulance to my apartment. We all checked Kelsey thoroughly, and then loaded her up in the ambulance. I went with the ambulance and rode to the emergency room about 20 minutes off of base. I was up there, walking around frantic as the EMS squad took her into the emergency room to get checked out. I knew that Leslie said that she would follow up to the emergency room, so I waited and waited on her. It must have been a good hour and a half before she got there. Cell phones didn't really exist then, like they do now, so neither of us had one to communicate with.

The next thing I see is 3 Prince William County police officers walk into the emergency room of the hospital escorting my wife. She looked quite shaken up, and dazed. I asked her what she was doing being escorted, and she told me that she had a wreck in the car. She had been in a rush, as frantic as I was, and ended up running a red traffic light and got broadsided by an oncoming car. It bowed our car in half like a pop can. If I wasn't freaked out enough by the fact that our daughter was possibly injured, then came the accident that also put more anxiety on me. All of the time I waited, even after Leslie got there, and I still hadn't heard anything from the hospital staff as to the status of Kelsey, how she was doing, her vitals or anything. If you have ever been to an emergency room at a hospital, you know exactly what I am talking about. Not only do you not want to be there, but it is an endless wait, everything moves slow, and you never get out of there at a decent hour. Finally the hospital staff came out to get us, around 9 AM and we went back into the emergency room. They had taken her for scans and had closely monitored her for any ill signs. They explained to us that she was perfectly fine, just a bit shaken up. Apparently, according to what they told us, babies are less prone to injuries than adults are, because they still have soft, flexible bones which are not brittle. There was not one single thing wrong with her. She was in perfect health! I was so relieved that my sweet light of my life was alright, and not hurt. It was a large weight which was lifted off of my chest, and thankfully also, Leslie wasn't injured.

Chapter 9 - My End of Enlistment

Skipping ahead slightly to the end of my Marine Corps, active duty enlistment I was due to end my duty on November 17th of 1999. Sometime during the summer months of 1999, I came home on leave from the Marine Corps to visit everyone, Leslie and Kelsey in tow. As you will read from the below excerpt of an email which my father sent to me, much later, recapping the part of the events, you will see why it was a mistake, and later while you read further, and the interesting thing is, the "fair" closes at 11PM. So where was she for 3 hours? Who on earth knows, but it didn't take nearly that long to drive from where she was "stating" she was, to where I was located.

"My wife and I have been concerned about Kelsey's care for many years. Her mother has done numerous terrible things over the years, in my opinion.

Before Kelsey was born, my wife, my mother and I spent one of the worst nights of our lives trying to sleep while she griped at Cleland all night. None of us got any sleep.

The nightmare started while Cleland was home on leave from the Marines. We were all staying with my mother who lived in Flatwoods. Leslie took Kelsey, who was a baby at the time, and said she was going to visit her mother. As the day and evening wore on, with no word from them, we became concerned. Cleland tried calling everyone he knew trying to locate her. No one knew where she was. She had Cleland's car, and Cleland borrowed my truck to drive while trying to find her and Kelsey. We all got more worried as the hours went by. It was after midnight and still Cleland couldn't find them.

She finally made it to my mother's around 2 am. She said she had been at the Scioto Co. Fair and that the time had gotten away from her. Kelsey was tired and I told Leslie she should be ashamed of herself for keeping Kelsey out so late and causing us so much worry. She took Kelsey and went on to spend the remainder of the night at her mother's. That's where the nightmare started.

Cleland went the next morning to get his clothes that were at her mother's. Cleland was planning on leaving Leslie and the baby at her mother's while he went back to Quantico. Cleland was getting out of the Marines that month and had to go back to base so he could get his base apartment cleaned and read for inspection while he was clearing post.

Cleland was soon to be discharged from the Marines. He had taken the State Police test and was hoping to get into a new class starting that January of 2000. The next thing we heard was she had filed a complaint saying Cleland had tried to run over her with his car the morning he went to her mother's to get his clothes.

I was in court the day the case was brought before the Judge. She told the judge the same story about Cleland trying to run over her with the car. The judge asked her if Cleland did anything else to her, and she said he hurt her arm. The judge asked how he hurt her arm; she said he hurt her arm trying to get her away from the front of the car.

She didn't realize she had let the cat out of the bag. It was obvious to the judge that she was standing in front of the car trying to keep Cleland from leaving and he was trying to pull her from the front of the car.

That false complaint cost Cleland a position with the State Police. They wouldn't hire him because of the domestic violence complaint. He was the victim."

Bob James

At the time, I was on temporary active duty, TAD for all of you veterans, to Officer Candidate School, MCB Quantico, VA, which was on the other side of the base, closer to Larsen's Gym, which myself and Leslie often visited. When we would both go to the gym, we would ask one of the other Gunnery Sergeants wives to watch Kelsey, so we could exercise. My job, while on TAD, was a company police sergeant. I was a Corporal at the time, holding the billet of a higher NCO. I was responsible for the organization of all platoons in the company, accountability of the candidates, who was training, who was on sick call, and intermediate training. I would go in on a daily basis and educate the candidates on procedure, alongside of the Drill Instructors, and ensure their safety, and make sure that their equipment was stocked, and issued. I was also responsible for collection of equipment, cleaning of equipment and restocking. Additionally, I took orders from the company commander, Captain Erikson, and the First Sergeant of the company. We also had a Gunnery Sergeant, who was subordinate to the First Sergeant, who scheduled the training regimen for the candidates.

I would do physical fitness operations with the candidates, as well as the Drill Instructors. My responsibility was to bring up the rear of the company while we were running to encourage, and push the candidates to get back up front. There were several times that I had to keep the candidates together, because after 5 miles running in full gear, the weight starts getting to you, especially in the summer months, where it is hot and you are sweating profusely.

So, just 2 short weeks before the end of my enlistment, Leslie, Kelsey and I, took what accrued leave (vacation days) I had, packed up some belongings and went back to Kentucky for a visit to get away. We went to her mother's trailer back on Plum Fork ridge. During this time, we drove around to visit family and friends, whom we hadn't seen in a long time, just to get reacquainted with them.

The evening prior to the end of my leave to go back to Quantico, Leslie and I packed up the car, put Kelsey in her infant car seat, and were preparing to leave. Again, I am not sure what the problem was, as it has just simply been way too many years ago, but Leslie and I started arguing again, and my mother-in-law was right outside with us, right in the middle of it. She didn't exactly butt into the argument, but she did something even worse and that was reach into the car behind my back while I was distracted, and try to extract my daughter from the car. I caught her trying to do this, and grabbed the lapel of her shirt, and pulled her out of the vehicle. I was already irritated with her daughter, and this didn't put me in a better mood. I warned her to leave her hands off my daughter.

Still the argument continued, and not more than a minute or two later my mother in law attempted to do it again. I firmly explained to her that if she touched my daughter again, I was going to under no certain circumstances break her arm. I simply was protecting my daughter in an aggressive situation, not to mention being forced to head back to base in a hurry at the last minute.

Somehow during the course of events, things calmed down enough, that I decided to stay a few minutes longer and relax before the long journey back. While I was waiting, Leslie took Kelsey back into the trailer. A very short while later, I had went back out to the car again to start it up and prepare to leave again. Leslie decided that she was going to block me from backing out of the driveway, so she stood behind the car.

I, bound by my duty to return to base on time, left the driver's door open, walked to the rear of the vehicle, grabbed her arm and pulled her out from behind the car. I may have been irritated at her, but I sure didn't want to hurt her. I walked back to the car and put one foot back in the driver's door. The next thing I see comes Leslie with a full size cinder block, you know the kind used for construction, and threw it directly at the window of my car. Thank God for a fast reflex is all I can say here. I already had the car in reverse, so I flopped down and hit the gas, backing out fast. I yelled out the window, because at this point I had all of her that I could stand, and told her she was crazy and she could just stay her butt right where it was. I pulled out and continued back to Virginia.

Chapter 10 - Scrub and Polish

Over the course of the next couple of weeks, I cleaned and cleaned on our base apartment to get it fully inspection ready for turning it back over to the base housing personnel. It was hours and hours of scrubbing, and gallons of water. By the time I was done with that apartment, Jesus Christ himself would have considered ordaining it and using it for the "Holy of Holy's". It was so clean, not even a speck of dust existed. Also, during the course of the next couple of weeks, I received my first Domestic Violence Restraining Order from our home town court system in Kentucky. This is where the proverbial shit really hit the fan. I ended my enlistment, and came home to Kentucky.

By the time I had ended my enlistment and made it home, my parents had done sold the house that I had grown up in. I was so used to being able to come home, and being able to sleep in my own bed, at the house that I was accustomed to living in. My mother and father had relocated to Florida, where they lived before I was born, so that they could enjoy the nice warm weather where they enjoyed living. They had moved to Kentucky after I was born in 1977, to raise me around family and to raise me in the country. I assume they figured since I was raised and out of the house at this point that they had nothing tying them to Kentucky, so they moved to where they wanted to.

I ended up moving in with my grandmother Lila, who was my dad's mother. You're probably wondering why I didn't move back in with my wife, right? It goes back to what I had previously mentioned, and that was because she filed a restraining order on me, from where I had went back to base. Barbara had warned me, and I was just seeing what she meant by telling me not to marry her. Well, it goes back to what I previously mentioned, and that was she filed a restraining order on me, through a domestic violence complaint. My mother and father worked a lot while I was growing up, so I spent a lot of time with mammaw.

She was like a second mom to me. She watched over me like a hawk. I couldn't make a squeak in that house of hers without her hearing it. I swear that woman had bionic implants, or supersonic hearing. She could be sitting in the living room and know when someone was outside of her house. There was nothing at all that got by her. She was the all Seeing Eye, if you will. She always made sure that we were fed, and comfortable. She was one wonderful woman, whom I could never repay in kindness, the way she did for me. Her house was cleaner than any hotel that you could ever stay at, and nothing was ever out of place. A dirty dish was never in her sink, because she washed dishes religiously.

She knew when you had something on your mind, she knew when something was wrong, and she could cook the most amazing food ever made. That was one amazing, loving woman whom I owe many thanks more than I could ever repay. I remember her saying to me, just like it was yesterday, "Bubby, are you hungry?" She always thought of making sure we weren't hungry. If it was up to her though, I'd be plump as a watermelon. I'm not sure if you were lucky enough to have a grandmother like this, but I was grateful.

I used to take my grandmother out on little dates, just me and her. My poor grandfather, who was an important person to me passed away not more than 6 months after my enlistment into the Marines. I remember pappaw telling me not to come rushing back on his account, at the time kneeling beside his bed, but I promised him that I would return in my Dress Blues. My grandmother was always so lonely when he passed on. She couldn't stand anything out of place. There isn't a hotel in the world that could keep their stuff cleaner than she did.

I have many memories of my pappaw. He, mammaw, my father and mother, and uncles all got together and built a log cabin. I remember sitting there and wondering around watching them work. I guess at the time I was 9 years old or so. Just like any curious kid, I was looking at the chainsaws, and circular saws, and my uncles and father kept reminding me that they were dangerous. What does a kid know anyhow? I didn't realize how dangerous they were, only that they looked interesting and that they could cut through trees. One picture that I still have is all of us sitting around the van my pappaw had while the cabin was still being built, so it is a pretty vivid memory for all of us.

Chapter 11 - The Passing of a Great Man

The day my pappaw passed away, I was on duty at the Provost Marshal's Office, not married yet, and the Lieutenant came to get me. I didn't know why he was asking for me, but by the time I made it into his office and saw the look of dread on his face, I immediately knew what he had to tell me. I felt like the world just fell through on me. I was so mad at myself for not being there by his side.

The lieutenant put me on administrative leave so I could return home for the funeral, and I returned home just as I had promised, in my Dress uniform. I respected my grandfather. He was not formally educated, but he was a brilliant engineer and mechanical genius in my opinion. He could figure out how to fix anything. He even designed and made his own rifles and muzzleloaders. He whittled his stocks from pure wood, with his pocket knives. His finished products were amazing, solid, and accurate. He used to bring home some of the best deer meat. I grew up on deer, squirrel and everything else he had. Nothing mammaw ever fixed tasted gamey and was always tender.

Ever since my grandfather's passing in 1996, mammaw stayed at home most all of the time. It was rare that she would ever leave the house, and when she did, it was at most for a couple of days at a time, and then she would scurry to get back to her house. I am not sure if she was afraid to leave the house, or if she missed the memories of my grandfather so much that she wanted to be right there with him even though he was no longer around. Just before I left for the Marine Corps in October of 1995, I remember kneeling at his bedside, talking with him. He clearly told me, "Son, don't come rushing back on my account." He had some years on him, and was not in the best of health, and I knew it. The stubborn man had been fighting diabetes for a long time, and he was going through dialysis 3 times a week. If you have had what I am talking about, or have someone in the family that you know who is or was going through this, then you understand that it really takes a toll on your strength, and your body.

He was going through dialysis for several months before his passing. He was a man of character, strong, and intelligent. He was not very educated, maybe an 8th grade education at most, but he was brilliant. He knew mechanics, electricity, and could build practically anything. One of his hobbies included building rifles and muzzleloaders. He would order all of the assemblies for the weapons, and build a stock to fit it, just as he wanted. He would simply start with a block of wood, and use his pocket knife to whittle down the stock. He would work on a stock for his newly designed rifle for months, cutting it to perfect size, shape, and design. By the time he was done with his product, it shot at perfect velocity, open sight, and accurate, although later he would always put a cross hair scope on it for long range hunting.

He would take his own weapons, his own reloaded ammunition, and go hunting. He hunted for everything, deer, squirrel, and rabbit. I grew up on this type of food at their house. It was not abnormal for us to eat a big stock pot of deer stew, or have deer burgers for dinner. My grandmother knew exactly how to season the meats, and it never tasted gamey. It was also tender, and way healthier than you could ever buy at a grocery store plus it was lean. If you are only used to eating beef, you should really try it. I am telling you right now, if you get a taste of deer, you will never go back to beef.

I remember that there was a lot of family at the funeral whom I hadn't seen in years; first, second and third cousins, uncles from both sides, aunts from both sides, and spouses of all. We all gathered to witness the passing of a great man, whom we all knew intimately. The man didn't pass a stranger, gave his time in aid of others, and sometimes to the point people would take advantage of his kindness. I bet you know people like that in the world as well. I know my father has told me many different stories of where people would talk my pappaw into working on their vehicles for free when he did mechanics work in his 40's.

Chapter 12 - Here We Go Again!

Ok, so I got a little off topic in the last chapter, but there was a clearly defined purpose for doing so, and that was to show you and paint you a picture of the family that I grew up in. Most of my family wasn't wealthy, but I come from a long line of farmers, and hardworking, honest, and would do anything for anyone type of people. We always go out of our way to help people, and if we have to charge someone for work, it's not a rip-off. I don't believe in taking advantage of people. There have been several occasions that I have found wallets, or money lying around, and I will do my hardest to track down the owner of the money. If it is money that I find outside of a business, I always assume it belongs to the business owner. If it is a wallet, I always look for identification. Well, you get the picture I am sure, I am an honest, no bullcrap kind of guy, and I love my family. What more is there to say you ask; a whole hell of a lot. Keep reading and you will find out.

So now back to the nuts and bolts of events. Months went by while I was living with my grandmother. I couldn't see my wife, I couldn't hold my daughter, or play with her, nor could I even try. I asked everyone I knew about what was going on with my wife and child Kelsey and most of the people whom I knew, who knew my wife, wouldn't tell me a darn thing. I don't know who or what they were protecting, but they were holding information regarding my family, and the safety of my daughter and that was wrong of them.

The next thing I find out is that my wife, again, is running around with another man. No wonder why no one would tell me what the hell was going on. They either didn't want to get involved when I would ask them, or they were too embarrassed by her behavior. By the time that I left to go back to base, she hooked up with another guy named Gerald. She was out all hours of the day and night running around with this guy, doing God only knows what, and where was my daughter? She was left at my mother-in-law's, instead of having her own mother watching out for her, caring for her, feeding her, and bathing her, or getting dragged around all hours of the night by her mother. It was a complete, inexcusable dereliction of duty to my daughter. I don't know what I was more pissed off at, the fact that "as far as I knew "at the time this was the second guy that she had cheated on me with, or the fact she was neglecting my daughter Kelsey. She had not a care in the world, as to the behavior she was exhibiting, and she didn't care who she hurt along the way. Leslie didn't have any interest, from what my family and I saw, in how she was parenting. All that Leslie had in mind, was getting what she wanted; and to hell with everyone else.

Months went by while I was fighting with the attorney to get into court about the domestic violence order that the judge was stupid enough to sign off on. In the meantime, this was also time which I was not allowed to see my daughter, and my wife knew it. I believe in my mind, that this whole situation was premeditated. I believe that she had this planned before I ever left the base to come home, and she was executing her plan step by step.

I ended up debating to no end with my attorney in the county, and finally was able to make it back to court. Once I got in court, I explained to the judge what had happened, and why it had happened. The judge then questioned my wife and was able to see right through the cloud of bullcrap that she had filled out on the domestic violence complaint. This caused the judge to sign off on a domestic violence order which was falsified. The judge was irate at the fact she clearly lied to him and was in the process of holding her in contempt of court and locking her up. I asked the judge to not do this, as I was a softhearted, kind person and didn't want my daughter to not have her mother around. If I knew what was going to be coming up in the following years, I would have let him lock her up and throw the key in the river.

Shortly after the dropping of the DVO, I, against all of my better judgment, wanted to again try and rekindle my marriage with Leslie. I talked to her friend Priscilla, since she and her husband were divorced, who was back in Kentucky and set up a dinner date, which my wife was to not know about. All she was to know was that she was getting dressed up to go out. I rented out the entire backside of one of the restaurants across the river in Ohio. I had fine China reserved, candlelight dinner, and entertainment. Yes, as ridiculous and this is going to sound to you I dressed up in a God Awful Genie costume to humor the girl, but it sure as heck was humiliating to me. What we do for the people we love. I tried to sit down over dinner and talk with her, and was able to do so, for a short bit. She got up and went to the bathroom and didn't come back in. I ran out back, and there she was sitting in Gerald's brown truck right in the parking lot and they drove off. How mad would you be? I was furious!

I there-in-turn filed for a divorce. I couldn't handle it anymore, the fact of my wife cheating on me every chance she got, and the fact that she was an aggressive person, who had no regard for my daughter's well-being. My attorney got busy on the paperwork, and pulled her into court. The bottom line of it here is that I had every right to take my daughter from my ex-wife and she knew it. As a matter of fact and record, she was told this sitting in the mediation room at the court. I didn't want to do that, again, because I had a conscious and couldn't bear my daughter not having her mother, but I agreed on joint legal custody with her as the custodian, and me as the non-custodian, so I could go to college and work. I always had a drive for bettering myself, and I wasn't about ready to let a wife who didn't give a darn about anything but herself do anything to slow me down. I was a father, and a good one at that, and my responsibility to my child was to set the example the best I could for her education and career wise. Not too many months after the divorce was finalized in mid-2000, Leslie said something to me that I swear I found funny. She said, *"If you hadn't filed for divorce, I would have come back to you."* She had to have had her head in the clouds. There was no way, no how, under any condition that I would ever in a million years take her back in my life letting her continue as my wife. She made her bed, and she could lay in it for all I cared at that point. I was done being treated bad by her. Somehow she thought she could just do whatever Leslie wanted to do and that she could come back to me and just pretend that it was my fault that she did what she was doing. That is the same game she has tried to play on me for years, and I couldn't handle her anymore.

Chapter 13 - Extortion

At the point of divorce, my daughter was about 2 and a half. She was the most beautiful thing you would ever see, and I was a proud father, but because of all of the drama my ex-wife brought with her, I didn't really get to see my daughter till she was about 3 years old. Leslie did the best she could to evade me seeing my daughter.

2. That since July, 2000, the Petitioner has been unable to exercise his visitation for the reason that he does not know the whereabouts or the address of the Respondent, ʼ, and he cannot obtain a phone number to contact her; that ˅ gave his family one phone number and when he tried to us it it was a number that he was never able to reach her by using.

3. That the Respondent has made it clear to this Petitioner and has engaged in conduct since their separation to defeat his visitation rights and has indicated that he will never visit this child.

I remember one time while my now ex-wife was moved back in with her mother in the old trailer, I was up visiting and they called the police. I ended up leaving and coming back to my grandmother's to just get away from them. I learned what Barbara was trying to tell me before we got married. Leslie was unstable, not to be trusted, and too wild to manage, and you know what, she was right in her advice, and I didn't listen, although it is clear that I should have.

My mammaw told me to avoid going out there by myself because of the known problems which I had been through because of Leslie. I listened to mammaw because she was watching out for my best interest. All of us knowing what had previously transpired, and the type of person I was and the background I had worked hard for, she wanted me to be safe, and to not tarnish my record in any way. All of us knew that because of my government work, I wanted to keep my record clear because of my clearance level. What can I say, but she was right on the money, and I honored my mammaw, so I listened.

It became a back and forth batting contest to see my daughter. Leslie started using my daughter as bait to get what she wanted from me. Not only did I have to pay child support, but she would frequently call me asking for money for any number of reasons. I was doing my due diligence by getting the payments in, so why should I give what little bit of money I had left. After all, she was the reason why I filed for divorce and she was the sole reason why she was struggling. It was my job to provide for my daughter, but she had equal responsibility and she wasn't even trying to get work, and it became clearly obvious to me that she was out burning the roads up. For the most part, my daughter was staying with my ex-wife's mother while all of this was going on. Now, if she was working and honestly wasn't able to make ends meet, and the money was to be used solely for Kelsey, I would have rendered aid, but she was all about running around and I wasn't going to support that. If I didn't "help" her with the extra money, she would make it difficult to see my daughter. If you ask anyone in my family, they would tell you that what I am saying is fact. Isn't that called extortion? As for what my mother and father have put up with, it is no wonder why we all haven't completely pulled our hair out. Here is another excerpt, from my father showing misuse of stuff that was intended for Kelsey.

"My wife and I have bought Kelsey many things over the years that have been misused or taken back for a refund. We bought Kelsey an electronic toy once that cost about $85 and her mother took it back for a refund. She has taken back clothes that we have bought Kelsey. We started washing the clothes we bought for Kelsey and cutting the labels out so she couldn't return them. We bought Kelsey a nice bedroom outfit with a student desk. They use the desk for a TV stand in the living room."
Bob James

There was one time, while I was on reserve duty in the Marine Corps, in Ohio that I bought a brand new $800 dollar Sony Vaio computer system, so that when I got back to Kentucky, I could give that to my ex-wife for my daughter's' school education when she got old enough to use it. Yes, I know it was a little early to get my daughter such an item, but as you can tell from reading, I am a planner who thinks way ahead of the curve. Later down the road, multiple times, I asked my ex-wife where that computer was, because I wanted my daughter to start using it to type up her reports for school, and do research with it. During the many times that I asked about the computer, not one time, could my ex-wife give me any type of answer as to the location of the computer system. I can't be totally for sure about this, but I sincerely believe that my ex-wife pawned it for money. If that was the case, why couldn't she come right out and tell me, which would be the intelligent and ethical thing to do. The same thing goes for the clothes, and items that my parents have purchased for my daughter over the course of the years. It has been noted that my ex-wife has taken the clothes back for return of money. It got to a point, where before my parents would send any type of clothes, they would cut the tags out, and mark my daughter's name inside of the clothes to prevent such action from occurring. Now I ask you this, should a person have to go to that extent?

I remember at one time, my ex-wife bought my daughter and her son a 4-wheeler to ride each. I would have never agreed with that, because of all of the accidents that kids have on them. It wasn't too long later, that that I remember my daughter telling me that her mother sold them, so she could pay the bills. Ok, first off folks, you don't buy your kid something that you're going to take back. Have you ever heard the word "abrogate?"

Chapter 14 - Off to College I Went

Sometime around the start of college shortly after summer break in 2000, I enrolled into Hazard Community College. I couldn't wait any longer to try and start educating myself, because I had let the spring semester pass by, as I was dealing with legal issues with my ex-wife Leslie over our daughter Kelsey. I figured the best way for me to really concentrate on my school, was to get away, so I didn't have any distractions and learn. I moved down to Hazard Kentucky and attended the community college there, studying Information Systems. I knew that I was going to be a perfect fit for that type of technical coursework, as my father was an Electronics Technician and knew about programming as well as computers and networks. This man, my father, single handedly built the network for the government agency he was working for at the time, as they never had a network beforehand. It was in my blood already, and he started teaching me, while he was attending school himself for his job, when I was 8 years old. He had me programming in basic computer language, binary, and a few other languages. He taught me a lot about circuitry, and most stuff an average 8 year old could care less about, alone get interested in, but somehow my dad made it fun for me.

I got so good at it, that I could literally write programs on an old TRS80 if you remember computers that old, and I could actually get it to compile and work. It was amazing to me that I was able to do things like that, especially at such a young age. This era of computers had used a 5 ¼ floppy disk, which looked like a piece of camera film, and was flexible, not like the later 3 ½ inch floppy disks which were in plastic. In today's time, no one would even care to waste their time with one of these floppies. It simply has no storage space, and programs we use today require a whole lot more than these floppies can help with. In any event, what I am telling you is that because of the encouragement of my father, I learned a lot at a young age, which was to help me in my later college classes, and my future career.

While at Hazard, I studied Information Technology, which is pretty much "everything you need to know about computer systems", so I could make sure to get a job in the technology field. I studied databases, networks and networking, programming in a variety of languages, e-commerce, web page development, and a whole lot of other aspects. It was a day and night experience for me. I would go to school, then come back to my apartment I had setup, and run labs on my own computer. I would tweak, and tweak it till I got it running perfectly. Some of my classes were day classes, while I also attended night classes. I will tell you right now, it was a full time load of classes.

During the course of my residence in Hazard, I would periodically drive back to my hometown to visit with my daughter Kelsey. It was about 2 ½ hours to drive up, so on top of my studies which I was already exhausted from, I took the time to come home to see my little baby girl. I would most of the time have to drive to mammaw's, and then rest up, call ahead and schedule a pickup, then drive again onto the ex-wife's mothers for pickup. It was a rarity that I ever got the courtesy of my ex-wife to meet me halfway. She always came up with some type of excuse that she couldn't. She didn't have the gas money, or her car wasn't working, or she had an appointment, or something that would get in the way of exercising her parental responsibility. I attended the school in Hazard till late in 2002, so by now Kelsey was rounding a little over 4 years old. You should have seen how beautiful she was.

During the time that I was going to school in Hazard, I was also back in the US Marine Corps reserves, as a Corporal, and I would drive up, one weekend a month, to Dayton, OH, where the Marine Corps Military Police Reserve unit was located. Keep in mind that I was already exhausted from my travels back and forth between Hazard and Greenup, Kentucky visiting my daughter; but I was also tired from constant classes at the college. In addition to traveling to Dayton, OH for my reserve duty, I was also holding down a job in Dayton, OH at a factory, where I would work during the weekends as well driving a forklift. I didn't get much rest at all during these 2 years while living in Hazard because of all of the events going on. As you can imagine, I was gone quite a bit, up to my ears in books, and holding down a job as well as military duties, and still managing to spend time with my special baby girl.

In 2001, during the summer, my father and mother drove up from Florida to visit mammaw, and see Kelsey. They stayed about 2 weeks, and I drove up to spend time with all of them. It was a good summer and dad took his granddaughter out, like he always has, to spoil her. It is a grandfather's prerogative if they want to do that, and besides, he wouldn't listen to me about overdoing it if I wanted him to. I just accepted that he wanted to do this for Kelsey, so I just stood back and let him do what he enjoyed doing and that was taking Kelsey out on every adventure he could, and letting him spend time with her, the way he saw fit, because after all, that was his granddaughter. On the way back to Florida, something odd happened to dad. He was driving and had to switch out with my mother, because his head started pounding so bad with a headache. By the time they reached Titusville, FL, mom had to take him to the emergency room at Parrish Medical Center, and he was admitted. After numerous tests, it was found that dad had contracted a bacterial strain of Meningitis, apparently from some pesky mosquito while he was in Kentucky visiting. This strain of Meningitis really did some damage on my father, as he was already diagnosed with Leukemia when I was 13, back in 1989. When my mother told me about his cancer in 1989, it really upset me, because none of us was sure that my father would be around very long.

Because of the Meningitis, on top of the Leukemia reducing my father's immunity, it set him into a coma. At the time, I was visiting with Kelsey in Kentucky, and I panicked. I wanted my daughter to see her pappaw one last time before he passed away, and I needed to be by his side as well. I took off, Kelsey in tow, and we both drove from Kentucky, to Florida directly to the hospital. I learned something very important during this trip however. Vehicles and food don't go together when you have a 3 year old with you. We stopped every couple of hours to get something to drink, and something to eat. Remember earlier when I was talking to you about cause and effect? This was one of those situations that I should have known better, but I was a young Marine at the time, young parent, and frankly it didn't dawn on me. After we made it halfway, Kelsey spewed all over the car. It was rank, and all over the back of my car. I ended up throwing away a whole set of my clothes, because it was all I had at the time to clean it with, but for dad and my daughter, I didn't care. There was only 1 objective in mind at that point in time, and that was to make it to my father's side!

Once we arrived in Titusville, made it to the ICU floor and walked in, a great deal of the family was already there; my mother, aunts, uncles, cousins, and friends from the churches, most of which from West Virginia and Kentucky. Until I could gage how the situation was, the family watched Kelsey so I could walk back in the back and see dad. When the nurses came out to get me, I walked back, and they led me to the room that my father was in. It was a sealed room, with glass sliding doors that was separated from all outside environment. They had my father on total, isolated quarantine. I had to put on sterile robes, and a mask to enter the room, and had to wash my hands and put on bacterial cleaner and gloves as well. I agreed to all of this, because it would have been terrible to introduce any further bacteria into the room where my father was at. He was in a coma at the time and wasn't aware of anything going on around him. He literally scared the crap out of me, because he looked just like my grandfather who had passed away a few years beforehand. His face, and body were swollen up, because of the fluid on his body, and he had tubes in his mouth for feeding, and IV's in his arms for liquid meds to be introduced for his care. I was an emotional train wreck right now, but because of my family, my father and my daughter, I didn't show any emotion at all, because someone needed to be strong for the sake of my father's condition.

My ex-wife completely flipped out over the fact I took my daughter to Florida. She didn't care not one iota about dad being in his condition, nor did she care if Kelsey saw him. So far, in all of the time that I had been exercising my duties for visiting my daughter, she had not 1 single time met me anywhere halfway, because she never had any money for gas, nor did she have a vehicle that worked well enough to make the attempt, or at least that was her excuse. I had to go 100% of the way to see my daughter when I wanted to. Guess what however? She got in the car, and I can't remember who with, but she drove all the way to Titusville, Florida to get Kelsey from the hospital, which was about a 17 hour drive. Amazing isn't it? She can't make an effort to help me see her 2 hours away, but she went well out of her way to retrieve "her daughter". After about 2 weeks of a lot of medical care, and prayers, my father woke up, and went home, which was a blessing to the whole family and a lot of prayers answered.

Chapter 15 - The Return to Ashland

I decided that I couldn't handle being away from Kelsey any longer, and I missed my mammaw Lila, so I closed up shop in Hazard and moved back in with my mammaw. I transferred my college credits to Ashland, so that I could continue my degree in Information Technology, be around family at the same time, and hopefully obtain a job. I figured that I had probably better spend more time with my grandmother, as she was getting older.

Just like before at hazard, the coursework was approximately the same, except I was able to transfer my credits in from the previous school, and continue on through my educational curriculum. Sometime throughout the school year of 2003, while using my Department of Veterans Affairs benefits, chapter 30, I ran out of benefits. Apparently there is some type of rule, governing education, which I was never informed of. I had a meeting with the president of the college, who granted my meeting with him, as his son was a US Marine as well.

In order to properly use my Montgomery GI Bill benefits, I had to attend school full time, which is what I have been doing at hazard Community College, and continuing through on Ashland Community College, for the Associate in Science for information technology. The problem that I ran into was that the full course load that I was taking, put me up against the wall, and I was no longer allowed to take any more courses at a two-year institution. The president of the college granted my request for a meeting, and we sat and discussed over a cup of coffee the problem and solution. He explained that in order to continue throughout my degree, I would have to move on to a four year institution, which would be a State University.

I ended up unfortunately having to take a break from my school, as it was right in the middle of the school year. In 2003, I enrolled in Shawnee State University, located in Portsmouth, Ohio, to pursue an advanced degree in management information systems. Most all of my credits transferred in from the previous associate schools. While attending Shawnee State University, I didn't take any technical courses. The classes that I unfortunately had to take we're general education - sociology, art, philosophy, things that I would never use in my field, but where required in order to get my diploma. These types of courses are considered general education or core classes.

While back living with my grandmother, I was able to visit my daughter on a more regular basis. I still didn't get any assistance from my ex-wife by being able to see my daughter. She never attempted to ever meet me halfway still, nor did she ever promote me coming to see my daughter.

Sometime about the time my daughter was 5 years old, I bought her a remote control Hummer truck, yellow in color, and I would take her out and let her drive the Humvee around. This was one of the ones that were about half the size that she was. There was a huge church right down the road from where my grandmother lived, so that there was a big parking lot in order for her to drive it around.

I even had fun driving it around with her. It was the same place that I had learned how to ride my bike when I was her age. My mom and dad would take me down there and help me learn how to stable my bike. Just like any child, they thought that they would never get the hang of it, because I know that I didn't. Wreck after wreck. It was fun spending time with my daughter, but I always worried about her. My dad always preached to me, to keep her from getting any scrapes scars or scratches, because he didn't want her being scarred for life and frankly I agreed with him. This caused me to always be on guard while my daughter was around, and I guarded her like a hawk 24/7. I was scared to death to let my little Kelsey get out of my sight, and I always was worried. Call me a worry wort, but as crazy as the world is that we live in, I wasn't going to take any chances.

While attending college, living with mammaw, I put my desk in her spare bedroom, along with all of my college books and technical manuals. For anyone who has ever attended college, you know the level of concentration it requires to study. Seeing Kelsey and juggling my studies were not an easy task. I remember how polite Kelsey was at this stage in her life. She would come to the door of my room and ask if she could come in. She would knock, and smile and work her way right over to my desk. She always was a daddy's girl, and I, a big daughter's daddy. I loved it, more than life.

Chapter 16 - Kelsey and her Schooling

To me and my family, education is paramount. In today's society, it's impossible to get a career position with only a high school diploma, much less for someone who doesn't finish school. It is even hard today to lock down a career position with a degree in the job field you have studied for. Due to the country's economic cut backs, corporations are laying off in large quantities, going to outsource companies overseas where they pay less money out in salary, reducing the bottom line. A lot of companies are even going to using contractors instead of hiring employees. This reduces the overhead costs for the companies, by not having to provide benefits to the worker. It provides a job for the employee contractor, but provides no benefits to the contractor. Some of the contracting companies do provide benefits, but they are few and far between. Most of the contracting companies, however, give the contractor an option to have money removed from their paycheck for the benefits if they want them; but it is usually expensive.

I have always been interested in my daughter's education, and teaching her new tricks. Like me, my daughter Kelsey, was a slow learner in elementary school. I worried about her being able to do simple math, and tried a few different tricks to get her to learn, which I will explain later. That is exactly how I broke through my educational barrier when I was younger. I taught myself mathematical shortcuts, completely bypassing the order of operations and I managed to get the correct answer about 99% of the time. I remember when I first came home from middle school and had my pre-algebra book. I looked at my father and said what is X, and he replied that it could be any number. I said, "Which number", and he told me that I had to figure it out. He hired a friend and neighbor of ours at the time who was a part time teacher to tutor me. After a while of intense studying, our friend Rachel managed to have a breakthrough with me, and all of a sudden I took off with my abilities in solving equations. From there, I got really good at science, chemistry, physics and a number of other scientific based genres. I was hoping that the same would apply to my daughter after some tricks in learning.

There were times, since I lived locally now, that I really wanted to be able to go pick up my daughter from school, so that I could take her out to do things. At the time my daughter was attending elementary school in Kentucky, but my ex-wife refused to put me on the pick-up list. I have no idea why my ex-wife has made it so hard over the years to let me pick up my own daughter from school. Even as my daughter got older and got into middle school, Leslie would not put me on the pick-up list. It really bothered me that I couldn't go pick up my own kid from the school in order to hang out with her. One year Leslie would put me on the list, the next she wouldn't, and me being the type of person I am, sticking with standards, I would have expected that she would have put me on that list on a consistent basis. I feel that it was intentional just to play the game with me. You can imagine how irritating it is to go pick up your child from school, and the school staff's not letting you do just that, because you are not on a pickup list. Even with joint legal custody, and them knowing it, they still gave me problems and wouldn't let me take my daughter with me. I have a big question here! What is the point of having court drawn papers, which specifically state that you are the parent, biological parents, with legal rights to your own child, whom can make decisions for your child, but not allow you to do something as simple as pick your own child up from school?

I remember as part of my daughter's education, along with most families and most children, you play games at home for fun and education. Monopoly is one of the most familiar games that families play. It teaches accounting, money, life, and is based upon how the economy trades property. Just like when you rent a building from somebody, you have to pay them rent on that property. One day in specific, much later, when my daughter was about 12 years old, Mary, my fiancée, and I were sitting in the kitchen with Kelsey playing Monopoly. My daughter landed on one of our properties, and she owed us rent. She argued with us to no end that she knew how to count money, and would not let us help her. It was a simple $35 in rent; however she could not count out the money. I told her that if she could not count out play money the correct way, then she had no idea how to count out real money, and this was to help teach her the how-to's of money. It got to the point during that game that I ended up putting the game up because I got so irritated with her trying to count money, and arguing with us the entire time. What is the point of trying to teach her when she didn't want to learn, right? I was pretty irritated with Kelsey, and told her flat out, "You are unteachable because you want to be unteachable", because she was arguing and didn't want to learn how to do this simple thing.

Throughout my daughter's entire school time, she has had a problem in reading comprehension, as well as math. I've always been a stickler for math, because it is the basis of science, and in my field, it's a requirement. Have you ever been to McDonald's, and ordered a sandwich or something, and the waiter behind the cash register not be able to count you out some simple change? God forbid that the cash registers not give them a correct dollar figure, or the cash register break down and cease working. Could you imagine someone not being able to count out the proper change? Well, I have been there and I have seen this on multiple occasions where I travel around, and it has not been the first time that has ever occurred to me. Just to be perfectly honest about it, I just didn't want my daughter being one of those statistical numbers of people who didn't know how to count simple change. If I were someone like that, I would be embarrassed to be caught out in public, but for some reason in today's society, being ignorant is acceptable. This type of ignorance would never be acceptable in China or Japan, where they put so much emphasis on the education of their children, because ignorance breeds problems.

Chapter 17 - Why Not Break The Rules, or At Least Ethics?

Our universe has a few definitives, so let's find out why to not break the rules. One of them is rules, another is common sense, and yet another is actions and consequences. Einstein was no idiot; his theory of relativity is practical common sense. For every action there must be an equal and opposite reaction which must take place, right? Let's take for example that you are walking down the interstate. You know that there is traffic on the road, and you know that the vehicles drive on the road at high speeds. You also know that your body cannot move as fast as a vehicle, right? Would it make any sense to you, to stand in the middle of the road knowing that there are vehicles coming at you? Any prudent person would say no, and the reason why is that you will get run over, hit and thrown and possibly killed. This is a good example of what common sense dictates.

Let's take an example rules for a moment. Rules and laws are put into place to keep things from occurring. Let's say that you're driving down a country road, and you're coming into a curve. Usually on most roads there is a warning sign on the side of the road, which is in yellow, which states the recommended speed for the curve. Some of the curves are nearly 90 degrees, so the recommended speed for some of them are approximately 35 to 45 miles an hour or less, in the curve. Would it make any sense to you to enter the curve at 70 miles an hour? No? Well why not? The simple answer to this is your vehicle will not be able to make the turn and you will drive straight through the curve, off the road, and possibly over a hill. In other words don't enter a curve faster than you can drive. This keeps you from wrecking a vehicle, hurting yourself, or someone else.

Let's now take a look at what consequences are now, again, using the example of driving too fast. You are in a rush, heading to work, and you are running behind. You are driving 75 MPH in a 55 MPH speed zone, weaving in and out of traffic. The next thing you know, you have a police officer behind you with his lights on and pulls you over. Why? Because you broke the speed laws and his job was to pull you over. The consequence for driving too fast is to receive a ticket. The same goes for anything else. There are good and bad consequences to every decision you make during your life, and sometimes, those decisions you make even affect the others around you.

Moving forward in time a very short bit, when my daughter was about 5 years old, of course my ex-wife was still with her boy toy Gerald. Oh, did I mention at this point that my ex-wife was living in a government housing project in the town that she was from - Yes. There are rules governing who can live there, who can come and go, and how long they can stay. There are also rules of how many people are allowed to live in apartments, since they are all a different size, to accommodate the size of the family. Gerald was living with my ex-wife and daughter for a very long time, not just a visitor. He wasn't supposed to be living with her, and Leslie brought it to my attention several times. Apparently after a while they were having "relationship" problems, because they broke up for the longest time. I was still trying my best to spend time with my daughter Kelsey, and one night my ex-wife invited me over to her apartment. I agreed, since it was convenient, there was a place to sit and talk, and my daughter was there at her place as well. That night, after my daughter was asleep, my ex-wife decided that she was going to come out into the living room, wearing not more than skivvies, and try to seduce me back to her bedroom. I don't know how to tell you this, but I lost my attraction to her, not only in physical appearance, but in mind and emotion. I didn't want anything to happen, and I ignored her attempts. I guess she, somehow in her mind, thought that it was "ok" to try and get me in her bed after all she had put me through at the time. I was almost tempted to run screaming out the door! It reminded me of an episode of the "Desperate Housewives", TV show.

<u>Chapter 18 - Graduation from Elementary School</u>

Time moves fast. The older you get, the faster time seems to go. Any elder person will tell you, I just don't know what happened to my life, as it seemed like yesterday I was a kid and now I am nearing the end of my life. My father tells me that a lot anymore, since he is in his early 70's now. I understand where the man is coming from, because just yesterday I was a child, and here I am nearing my 40's. Life is short and goes by at the blink of an eye. Children just don't seem to understand how fast until they reach that point in their life to see their own life flash before their eyes.

I was so proud to be Kelsey's father. She was really doing much better in school and was finally at the end of her tenure at the elementary school. You should have seen how precious my little girl was in her red dress and dress shoes. She looked like a Disney Princess walking around, and boy was she proud and smiling. I can't say I blame her! It was a huge milestone in her life that she was just getting ready to overcome. Often, while you are in the making of your goals, you never think that you are going to finish - time just drags on. She finally made it up the first hill in her life, and now she was standing on top of it, ready to move forward in her life and tackle the next big thing to come her way. Wow, let me tell you, it was hard for me as her daddy to be standing there, knowing that she was graduating elementary school - but I was still proud. I took many pictures that day on my mobile phone, but my phone decided to have a thermal meltdown not only a few days later, so I lost everything. I was so darn mad at my phone that I pitched it and went and got a new phone.

No matter what you do in your life, keep in mind that first, enjoy the time that you have, and second, remember that you will get to your goal if you work hard enough. Just don't throw your time you have away, because later down the road, you will regret the things you walked away from, and what then? Can you go back? No. Can you repair some things in your life? Possibly. Can you move forward and do your best to remember what is important? You bet you can! Just like when Kelsey was younger, playing Monopoly with her, trying to teach her how to count numbers and money. I was helping her with her school, and she didn't even realize it. Sometimes children get extremely mad at their parents, for saying or doing things, but there is a good reason behind why. Lord knows I got mad at my parents when I was growing up, but I realized that they knew what they were talking about, or had a good reason for making me do certain things. I get it now as an adult, but boy did it drive me crazy as a kid.

Chapter 19 - Florida, Not the Ultimate Getaway

In the middle part of 2004, I moved to Florida, so that I could be closer to my parents. Although I missed my daughter Kelsey who was 6 at the time, my mammaw, and my friends, it was something that I had to do. In Kentucky, there simply wasn't much work, if any, in my field of expertise. If I did get a job doing what I do, I would be making nothing in the line of income, so logically; I would have to move to where the real companies were at, technology wise, in order to obtain a position where I could utilize my knowledge to make real money. If you look at Florida, or know anything at all about it, you will know that the west coast of Florida, around the Gulf of Mexico is an industrial area, full of factories, imports and exports businesses and lots and lots of real estate. On the east coast, you have NASA, Daytona Beach, Cocoa Beach, Ft. Lauderdale, and Tourist Destinations. The east coast is more where the fun is, but you also have major companies there that are right in my field, so they need people who know what they are doing.

As soon as I moved down there, staying with my parents, I enrolled into an online institution for college to see if I could finish out my degree. While I was doing that, I got a job with my father, who was now retired from his government job, who worked for the cruise lines around Titusville. Their responsibilities included making sure that passengers were being guided into the right terminals, ensuring that no weapons were allowed on premises, and assisting the Port Authority with any other security measures. Another part of our position included clearing the terminal and ensuring no suspicious baggage was left behind, and if so, to report it to the Port Authority, Coast Guard, and local Sheriff's Office.

If it was one thing I didn't do, was to move down to Florida to party. It was business up front and business in the rear. I didn't have time to do a lot of playing, and most of my time was either spent studying or working. While working armed security with my father, sometimes we would work 12-13 hours, and that gave me some time to study since a lot of my time was spent waiting. I am sure you have seen jobs like that, right? Anyhow, one of the posts we manned was a guard building, and there was not much traffic that came through there in the middle of the night, so I took textbooks, and my laptop, so that I could really crack down and learn even more. You can bet your butt that I sure didn't want to be away from my daughter, but it was the only way that I was going to be able to provide for her, and there is this little thing called money that the world seems to revolve around.

Not too long after I was there, traveling back and forth to Kentucky to visit my mammaw and my daughter Kelsey, I met a very nice, beautiful girl named Mary, who I started talking to. We hit it right off. Honestly, I never thought that I would meet another girl who I would fall in love with, because my ex-wife had treated me like such garbage, and lied and manipulated me to no reproach; but I took a leap of faith and decided to get to know her. I would either drive up from Florida to meet with her, or down from Kentucky. The first trip, I remember, was the most challenging one I ever faced. At the time I was at my mammaw's visiting and I drove down to see her. It was the first time that we ever physically met, although we had spoken on the phone quite a lot and exchanged pictures. It took me forever to get down to her local area in Tennessee. At the time, it was winter, and when I left Kentucky, it wasn't all that bad, but by the time that I had reached the Virginia state area, it was snowing so hard, like a blizzard, that I couldn't see 2 foot in front of the car. The roads were collecting snow really fast, and at one point, I was driving 15 MPH, just because I couldn't see and the roads were packed with the cold white ice. It was really dangerous but once I commit to doing something, for anyone that knows me, come hail or high water, I am going to carry it through if it kills me, and that is exactly what I did. I remember it was really late at night once I finally arrived, and she and her aunt met me at one of the local fast food restaurants in Tennessee. I couldn't believe my eyes that she actually showed up. The first thing when she stepped out of her aunt's vehicle, I fell right in love with her.

After that day, I would come up periodically and visit with her, and we would go out to the movies, or play putt-putt golf, or any number of things just to get out of the house. At the time, she was working for a local gas station as a clerk. She not only did the regular gas station duties, but they also had food preparation for customers, where they have hot-dogs, sandwiches, subs and the like. Her area in TN has a lot of truck drivers who pass through here, and local truckers who work in this area. Most of them would stop in at her gas station for coffee and snacks in the morning before hitting the road. On several occasions, I would visit her at work, and sit quietly at one of their dining room tables off to the side drinking coffee while she was working, and when she had time, she would come over to me and talk. It would always give her company so she wasn't alone at her work, and it would give me time to relax and shoot the wind with her. This went on for about 6 to 8 months, and then we decided that she was going to move down to Florida with me.

Chapter 20 - The Start of My New Life

It was then, when Mary moved down to Florida, that things really started to take off for me. I was still living with my parents, and mom did her best to accommodate us. It wasn't the most comfortable setup in the world, but it sufficed for what we needed at the time. Mary and I were staying in my mother's sewing room, and let me tell you, it was tiny. On one side of the room was my mother's work table with sewing machine and supplies, and on the other, racks on the wall holding rolls of materials of all colors and a clothes rack where there was a variety of clothes hanging down. We didn't have a bed in that room, so we threw pillows down on the floor and slept like that, but at least it wasn't a hardwood floor, it did have carpet and some padding. Thank goodness, because otherwise, our backs would have killed us. I remember waking up many of a morning, and the clothes were hanging 6 inches from our noses. Yes, I know it sounds funny, strange, and cramped and I agree, it was. Mary still laughs about that from time to time.

Not too many weeks went by and we located ourselves an apartment about 15 minutes away from my parents' house. It was a blessing, and honestly, it wasn't much bigger than moms sewing room, but it was big enough for me and Mary. The apartment had a kitchen, living room, bathroom and bedroom. The bedroom was so small, that our bed barely fit in the room. There was maybe a foot between the bed and the wall at the foot of the bed. In order to get in it, you had to crawl over the other person or scoot over. The kitchen wasn't that big either, and the washer and dryer were more or less attached to the kitchen counter. There was barely any closet space, and it was even a challenge to find anywhere to put a dresser for our clothes. Getting maintenance there was a huge deal as well. Although there were maintenance personnel, they would take their sweet time getting around to fixing anything.

I remember that we had routine problems with the air at the apartment. Remember, this was Florida, so we rarely ever had a need for heat. There was also a problem with the telephone wiring in the apartment. I got tired of waiting on the maintenance person one day, and grabbed my own telecommunications tools, and rewired the phone wiring myself, just so I could mount my phone on the wall. It wasn't even my responsibility to do so, but I figured, "if you want it done right, do it yourself." Once I was done with it, it worked like a charm; and I was able to finally mount my phone over there.

One of the biggest nuisances of the apartment complex was a younger maintenance guy named Scott. He constantly stared at Mary, and I got the feeling I couldn't trust this guy. Normally I don't have a problem with people, but this guy really gave me an uncomfortable feeling. At apartment complexes, they are supposed to knock on the door before entering, or give notice of when they are going to come fix something due to a work order request. One day, while I was gone to work, Mary was in the shower getting cleaned up, and when she got out of the shower, she rounded the corner into the living room, towel on, and there Scott stood in the living room working on the air. I don't remember what all Mary told me about that, but I guess he left.

Several weeks went by and we still lived there, and I was outside working on Mary's car, doing routine maintenance on it, so to keep it in good running condition, and he was doing his rounds. She was standing out there with me, talking, while I was working and I was under the car, and could see him walking fairly close to the car. I was just expecting him to say something since he couldn't see me easily. I imagine what it looked like, the hood was up and she was looking down into the motor like something was wrong. Mary didn't really need the car, since I had mine, but it was nice for her to go places while I was at work. She was working for a local department store which was less than a mile from our apartment, so she would normally walk or ride the bike to work.

Not too long after getting our apartment, I found a technical job working through a contract agency out of Palm Bay, Florida for a company called Harris in Melbourne. I took on a position for 18 months as a technical helpdesk analyst and we supported the internal staff around the world. It was not uncommon for us to get a call from someone in Africa, or Canada, or the United Kingdom. All of the staff we could clearly understand as they were English speaking, US Citizens, who happened to either be physically working in those geographical areas, or would fly to those areas for assignments. On many cases, I have had someone tell me they couldn't get to their computer, because there were literally lions in the road. At first, I thought these people were just pulling my chain, but in fact they were serious. I remember getting all kinds of weird, off the wall calls from these people. One guy I used to call the whistler, because he had an ear piercing shriek of a whistle every time he spoke. I am not sure if he had a gap between his teeth that was catching wind as he spoke or it was something else, but he did it every single time.

I was also a member of the Hurricane Response Team for Harris Corporate and I volunteered for this position. The objective was when a hurricane was due to hit Florida, and everyone was supposed to be evacuating the state, we would stay behind on lockdown, in the building which was rated for extreme winds, and not leave. There were backup generators at the facility, and our job was to keep the Harris world running when there wasn't anyone else that could. On one occasion, August 25th 2005, we were called in due to Hurricane Katrina making landfall; and it was coming right across Florida, through Orlando into Melbourne, FL, before making its way back out to sea. We were stuck in the building overnight, and I remember going downstairs and watching the Palm Trees bent clean over touching the ground; debris from every which way flying around. Winds reached approximately 120 MPH sustained and killed a lot of people and did a huge amount of damage. I remember leaving after the hurricane, and the roads had debris all over the place, power lines lying in the roads, and buildings knocked down.

Sometime in August of 2006, while I was still working with Harris, Mary got pregnant with our first child. We were both shocked, because we couldn't imagine how this could have happened. We couldn't figure it out. Somehow, someway it was meant to be. Actually we did know how this happened, just a little humor, but we were excited to have a new addition to our family. We didn't have any clue yet how we were going to make sure the little one had everything that it needed, but we were going to make it happen, with a little help from God, and a lot of hard work. Only time would tell.

Around this same time, my mother and father came up for a visit from Florida, to spend some time with Kelsey. They picked Kelsey up and went to my mammaw's, which is my father's mother, to stay, and brought Kelsey there with them. My father was shocked to find out what Kelsey had told pappaw while he was spending time with her over the summer.

"Many things have happened over the years to call into question Leslie's ability to provide a safe place for a child to grow. When Kelsey was about 8, she said she was in a car with Gerald (Leslie's new husband), the adults were drinking beer, and

they saw a cop and were afraid he would get them. My wife checked public records about the time this was going on and found that Gerald had been charged with drug possession and that Dorothy, the other grandmother, had been charged with shoplifting in Scioto County. Not the kind of people who should be watching a child. Kelsey is often left with Gerald or her grandmother."

Bob James

Not only was this a matter of public record, but also it was found out that Gerald had been fired from his job repossessing vehicles. It was discovered a piece of paper that my daughter had in her backpack at the time that she came over for a visit, that Gerald had allegedly stolen a chain from the gate at the vehicle yard. I didn't know anything about this, until I was informed by my father whom had that piece of paper. From what I understand, from my father, she was using this piece of paper for scribbling. It is amazing what a child can tell you, without them telling you anything.

Chapter 21 - Will I Ever Get Home to Kentucky

One can hope right? My contract with Harris lasted 18 months, and I had hoped to get hired on full time with the company as a regular employee. I had worked with one of the security team engineers in Harris to prove my worth, but what it boils down to is the bottom dollar figure. If the company is going to be able to save money, they are going to do just that. On December 24th of 2006, the contract for me ended, and they didn't hire me, so it was time to move on. Luckily enough, I had met another contractor who was to become a very good friend to me. I took him under my wing at Harris when he first came to work there after me, and he mentioned working for another company there in Florida. I gave him my resume, upon mentioning that to me, and told him, if you can do something with it, I would appreciate it, but if not, that is ok as well. He left Harris before I did to go back to work for his previous company. A week before my end of contract, I got a call from his supervisor at the other company asking me if I was still looking for a job. Absolutely I said.

I went over to meet with this supervisor and we hit it off, right off the bat. It wasn't even a standard office meeting. He and I met up after work outside in the parking lot, chewing the fat. He was a Marine as well, was Military Police as well, and worked for the same supervisor I did at Harris, who wasn't well liked, even by him. We had nearly everything in common, including liking to help people. He queried my technical knowledge, my ability to learn, and my abilities to follow through. I wasn't lying either; I told him that I catch on fast, absorb things like a sponge, and remember them, especially after having hands on. He said that he would see what he could do about getting me on with the company but no promises. I also informed him that I was leaving the state heading back to where Mary's family lived in Tennessee, so she would be able to see them.

Mary and I packed up our rinky-dink apartment, and moved our stuff back to Tennessee where her family lived. I kid you not, not a month went by, and I get a call from this supervisor asking me if I still wanted the job, and when I could come to work. I was absolutely thrilled to hear that news, and so was Mary, as she quit her job to move back to Tennessee with me, and neither of us was employed at the time. We turned around and moved, some but not all, of our stuff back down to Florida again so I could get to work with my new company Dictaphone Corporation. I bet you have heard of that company. Dictaphone is renowned in their products and solutions for customers. A great many police departments used to use Dictaphone for recording their inbound and outbound calls for record. A great many attorneys' offices used to use the same technology. Additionally, they had solutions for attorneys and doctors to leave dictations for transcriptionists to type. We moved back in with my parents again, till we could get things situated. It seemed like a pinball game bouncing around.

I went to work for this company, got a desk not too far away from this amazing supervisor's office, and right beside my friend who got me on. It was the perfect scenario, so I could learn from my friend, since he did that job before, and so I could get the hang of things. My supervisor wanted me to take 2 weeks and sit with and learn from my friend. I sat there less than a week and got bored, so I went over to my desk, dialed it up and got to work. What better way to get your feet wet than to jump right in the lake. I learn better when it's trial by fire, instead of a little at a time, it's more all at once. Just like in Harris, my call volume and call resolution went through the roof. I wouldn't let a ticket get by my desk without solving the problem, and I treated each and every person that called in like family. These, however, were not internal customers but external customers from hospitals around the United States who used the company software for healthcare. I had my hands full and I loved it. It was the job I was looking for; fast paced lots of responsibility, challenges to overcome, and goals to meet. When I get a job, I don't want something that I get bored with; and I sure don't want to sit there and not earn my keep. Call me strange, but I like earning my money.

In early May of 2007 something miraculous happened. We were doing our continued software educational training in one of the several training labs down stairs in the building I was working in. I met several of the field engineers in the company, who were both teaching the classwork, as well as attending the classes. I also met several of the other remote helpdesk people who I worked with on the phone, but never got a chance to meet in person, but I did that week. One day during that week triggered the next 9 years of my career. There was a guy who I had seen at the complex before but had no idea who he was, and he was standing out in the hall talking to some of the guys that I was in class with. I didn't approach him right off, because I didn't know who he was, until I heard him say something about Kentucky, and I went out there and jokingly said what's that about Kentucky?

He and I started talking and he mentioned that he was looking for someone to go back to Kentucky to fill a role as a Regional Field Service Engineer for the company. I laughed and told him that I grew up in Kentucky and had family there still. He said, "Do you want to go back to Kentucky?" I said, "in a heartbeat!" Instead of me going back to the class after my break, he snagged me out in the hall on my way back in and we went into one of the other adjacent training rooms and talked for a good long time. After which he said that he would see what he could do. After class was dismissed, I went back upstairs to my desk to log in and work, and my current supervisor came out to me telling me that the Vice President of the company wanted my resume on his desk right now. Let me tell you something. I have never seen progress being made as fast as that happened. It only took me 2 minutes to walk upstairs, and the VP already wanted my resume on his desk. That is the fastest thing I have ever seen happen in my life.

At the time, Mary was still at her mother's in Tennessee, until I could secure some place to live; but things were moving so fast that she didn't get a chance to move back down to Florida with me. I worked it out with Dictaphone, who was at that very moment being acquired by Nuance Communications to allow me to move back to Kentucky; and they were going to pay for a hotel for me for 2 weeks, to allow me time to find a place to live. My whole job for a 2 week period was to find a residence to live. After a lot of searching, I found a really nice, but expensive, apartment complex in Louisville KY. I didn't really want to be 3 hours west of my daughter Kelsey; because that just meant more and more driving for me, but I didn't really have a choice in the matter. The Nuance Company wanted me to be within a certain radius of Louisville, so that I could take care of one of their more challenging, needy customers, who were having a really hard time adapting to the Nuance line of software, and had not had a specialized field engineer local to their location for fast response time. Up until my time with the company, the closest engineer was in Atlanta Georgia, and it took a significant amount of time for him to reach the area.

On May 30th 2007, our child was born in Kingsport TN. What really put a damper on the whole thing was that I was up to my ears in work in Louisville KY working with Nuance at the time and I missed the birth of my child. Mary and I found out that it was going to be a bouncing baby boy, and I was thrilled, because now, I had someone to carry on my family name. What was another damper, was that because I wasn't there, and we weren't yet married, that he was to take on the Johnson family name, but I was still happy as a father could be, because now I had a son to pester, play with and enjoy. James James was born, and he was named after my amazing grandfather, Red, who passed away years before.

After finding the apartment, Mary moved up to Kentucky from Tennessee with me. I was so glad to have her back with me up there, because it had been 5 months since I had seen her after going to work with Nuance in Florida. This apartment was roomy, unlike our apartment in Florida, and was around 1600 square foot - practically the size of a medium sized house. I was thinking to myself, how awesome it was to be back in the Commonwealth of Kentucky, because then, I could really do what I wanted to do, and that was spend every chance I could get with my amazing and beautiful daughter Kelsey. That girl meant the whole world to me, and my life revolved around the little thing. She always did have me wrapped around her little finger and lets just put it this way, she always had a way to make my heart melt; how could you not be in love with something as adorable, fun, smiley, and giggly as that. At this point my daughter was about 9 years old, and was still living with her mother and Gerald. It never was one of my points of interest, but I think that Leslie and Gerald got married around this time.

Chapter 22 - Back in Kentucky, Finally!

I remember at this time, in the living room, at the new apartment we had our new son James, crawling around on the floor and enjoying himself playing with his toys. He couldn't have been any more than about 4 months at the time. It was fun lying on the floor of the living room playing with James. It was hard to believe that we had a new son.

In the living room of the new apartment is where I set up my office. I had acquired a desk, and brought my computer with me from Melbourne Florida, from my desk at the Nuance Company. I remember working for hours at a time, on the phone constantly, and traveling around taking care of customers. The company had issued me a Blackberry, which was tied into my company email, and I monitor it closely for assisting customers.

At the point of us living at the apartment in Louisville, but there were times where my father would come up from Florida, pick up Kelsey, and bring her to the apartment in Louisville, so that we could all spend time with her. There were also times that my father had brought my mammaw as well so that she could spend time with us. I was excited to be back and Kentucky so that I could do this.

Mary has reminded me that there have been a lot of times that we would travel to Eastern Kentucky where my daughter lived, at the apartments where my ex-wife lived, to pick her up. It was very rare that I would ever go to pick up my daughter by myself, as I would either have my grandmother, a friend, or Mary with me at pretty much all times. It was rare that we would ever bring Kelsey back to our apartment by ourselves. It was just too long of a drive from Louisville Kentucky, and we didn't want to waste a bunch of time by spending too much time driving on the road, and now, we had our son taking with us.

We would take Kelsey out to Gattiland to play games, to the dairy shop, to the park, out shopping, out to many different restaurants, and a variety of other things, simply to let her experience new things. We really enjoyed spending time with her, because she was really important, and we wanted her to spend as much time as she could with her new brother. For Mary and me, it was enjoyable to see the amazed look on her face, as she was seeing things that she never got to see before.

On one specific occasion, while I was working at my grandmother's in Kentucky, Mary took Kelsey down to drive her remote controlled Hummer, at the church just down the road from my mammaw's. Mary noted that there was a car parked in the parking lot, containing an old lady, and she was just simply sitting there with the car off. Mary warned Kelsey to keep the remote control vehicle away from this old lady's car, because it stood a good foot and a half high. Just like any kid, she didn't listen, and ended up plowing right into the side of this vehicle at full bore. Mary said that this old lady, not only didn't hear anything, but didn't even twitch. There was no turning of the head, and I don't even think she blinked. For all Mary knew, she could have been dead sitting there. I doubt that at all, because she later left, but that lady didn't even know that the world around her existed.

During the summer, Mary, James, and I went to pick up Kelsey for the summer break. She was 9 at the time, and she accompanied us on a trip to Florida to visit mammaw and pappaw, Bob and Linda, my parents. While we were down there, mammaw and pappaw watched James for the day, and I took Kelsey and Mary to Universal Studios. I don't think that place ever gets old, because of how much there is to do there, where the movies come alive for us. Of course we can see movies on TV, but there is just something exhilarating to be on a ride or in a theater where the reality is right in front of you. One of my favorite rides was the "Back to the Future Ride" where you were sitting in the Delorean, and you were chasing Biff flying through the air. Another one of my favorite rides was Twister, from the movie "Twister". This ride you actually just walked out onto a platform, and there was a scene of a farm, and they would spawn up a tornado right in front of you, out on the set. It couldn't have been more than 15 feet from you, and there was stuff flying through the air, and wind blowing hard, and the floor you was standing on shook. I remember that it scared the living daylights out of Kelsey, as she started crying and bawling out loud. The poor little thing, even though we told her what to expect when we went in there, couldn't handle the events happening right in front of her. Once we got done in the evening, Mary and Kelsey posed for me in front of the Universal Studios Globe sitting next to the bridge at Universal, at night. They looked so awesome together, and were both really having fun. Once we got done with that, we headed off to the Hard Rock Cafe to get something to eat before heading out of the park for the night. I don't know if you have ever been to eat at the Hard Rock Cafe, but wow, the prices were out there on the moon somewhere. For a hamburger, it was like $15 dollars, for fries another $5 dollars and a drink yet another $5 dollars. Anyone could go to Wendy's or McDonalds and eat a whole meal for $5 dollars, but here, it was around $25 dollars for a "value" meal. For 3 of us to eat, I spent somewhere in the ballpark of $80

We lived at the apartments in Louisville for right at about 1 year. When our lease was up, we decided that we're going to buy a house. I went to one of the local realtors in Shelbyville Kentucky, and sat down in his office to talk with him. Again, it was funny, because of what was about ready to happen. Here I am sitting in his office, looking around, and I noticed a lot of pictures of pretty much everything, except one of them stuck out like a sore thumb.

There was a picture, of a military unit, sitting on his desk. At the time the realtor was sitting behind his desk in his office chair, looking on his computer for a solution for me. I leaned forward, and took a good hard close look at the picture and noticed that it was a Marine Corps unit. I asked the realtor who was in the picture, and he told me that his son was a Marine. I took another look at the picture, and chuckled, it was my old unit - Military Police. The first time I looked at the picture I wasn't really concentrating on it that hard, but this time that I looked at the picture, there I stood right in the front row. Apparently, I was his son's Sergeant, and I didn't even realize it, until just then!

I ended up laughing about it with the realtor, because I didn't know and neither did he. He really did me justice by helping me out, at that point. I explained to him that I had about a week, on a strict deadline, in order to make a decision on a house. He took the time out of his schedule to look up all of the MLS listings he could, and we went out on a house hunting spree. In less than a half a day, we looked at over 10 different houses, and must have drove at least 30 miles total in the radius I laid out for him. He was able to restrict a search within the limits of where I wanted to live, and we got to work. I took a pen and a piece of paper with me and made lots of notes on every house. Some of them had good qualities; some of them had bad qualities, some of the needed repairs while others didn't need any repairs. By the end of that day, I knew exactly which house that I wanted to buy.

The house that I found was located directly across from an elementary school in Shelbyville Kentucky, and I mean within 200 feet of the school. It was the perfect place, since my son was about 5 years old at the time. We knew that he would be attending school in short order, and it would give me the ability to work from home, be home with him during the evenings, spend time with Mary, and all at the same time, walk him to school, or drive him to school if the weather was bad. It was really a good plan, good setup, and gave me a lot of conveniences from home.

Chapter 23 - A New Home

At this time, it was around August of 2008, Kelsey was 10 years old, and here we were, finally in our new home. Mary was still in Tennessee at the time with her parents, as she has just given birth to our son James. We figured it best that she stay there, in a stable environment, at least for a few months, until James was old enough to travel, and Mary wasn't sore anymore. It is always hard on a birth, along it being her first child, and even then, for a mother taking care of a newborn. By having her parents close by, at least for the time, it would make it much easier on her, and besides, I had my hands full preparing her home for her arrival.

When we bought the house from the realtor he had informed us, since it was law anyhow, that there was a suicide in the home, just the year beforehand. Things like that used to bother me, but after the Marine Corps, it was just another day. I never did get a chance to tell Mary about it, until after she had moved into the house, and it was something, at first, that bothered her, but after a short bit she learned to accept it, after all he was a human, not some alien that was never heard of before. I learned a lot about the guy who owned the house. When we moved in, the house was only 3 years old, and owned by only 2 people, the person who had it built in the sub-division, and the previous owner who was no longer alive. The previous deceased owner was in his mid-30's, and he was a Geologist for the University of Louisville, and the University of Kentucky, and did Geological research for both campuses. From what I understood, he did the research as part of agriculture surveys, but I can't be sure of that. I just gathered information from some of my surrounding neighbors, while I was asking them how well they knew the previous owner. Apparently, he was a really nice guy, and kept to himself for the most part, but of course being a Geologist, he didn't have much time to mingle given the research he was working on.

When James was around 4 months old, around September of 2007, Mary joined me in Kentucky and settled right in. By that time, I had James's bedroom setup, the house filled with furniture, my office organized, the garage setup, and the kitchen ready. Since this wasn't my first rodeo with a child, like it was hers, I already had a variety of baby things ready to go. I hate going into a situation guessing and not being prepared, so I was ready for this go around. Mary and I had picked out a crib for the little one, and it was built like a tank, and as a matter of fact, I still have it put up today. I don't get rid of too many things unless I need to, besides maybe one of these days, I might be able to pass it on to someone who needs it or even my grandbabies when that time comes. I like thinking years down the road, not weeks or months. It is the only true way to get prepared for the future. A lot and I mean *A LOT* of younger people in today's society live for the moment and never prepare for what is ahead of them; and that is why so many younger people get caught off guard with life. I am sure you know what I mean, and most likely, you have seen this yourself.

Now that we had our own home, that meant that we had our own buffer space, our own privacy where neighbors are not on the other side of the wall, and we had a back yard where we could have picnics, cookouts, tents, fire pits, or whatever else we wanted to put out there. At this point, we had a place where Kelsey could come, visit during our weekends together, and holidays, or any other time that she wanted to visit. I always wanted to see the little thing, because after all, she was my baby girl, and she was also the love of my life. If you will remember, she was always the light of my eye ever since she was born. She has had me tied around her little pinky finger, and as far as she was concerned, the world revolved around her. If you would have seen how we were together, you would have understood how important she was to me!

Mary and I would go down and get Kelsey quite a bit, and bring her back to our new home. It was a good area, and Louisville wasn't far down the road either. Sometime around this time, I got an annual membership to the Zoological Society, so I could take whomever I wanted, whenever I wanted to, to the Zoo, and it not cost me anything above and beyond what I had already paid for it, besides, a lot of people would be proud that I was supporting the animals and helping the society at the same time. I would take sissy to the Zoo and we would walk around and look at the animals, and get drinks and just play and talk. I thought that was the best time ever getting to hang out with my kiddo. She always did love animals, the same as I did, so that was a perfect time for us. One winter, and I mean it was cold, we went to the zoo and it was so cold that they had the Polar bears put up, if that tells you how cold it was. We couldn't stay very long, although we certainly tried, and eventually gave up and got back in the car. Have you heard the expression, "Colder than a well digger's butt in the winter", because that's how we both felt!

The Christmas of 2008, Mary, James and I made a trip to my grandmothers in Eastern Kentucky. We had arranged with Leslie to go get Kelsey for Christmas. There was no snow on the ground, but I do remember it was pretty cold, and it was a weekend when we showed up. My son was still getting used to riding in a car, but he was doing much better, although we had to stop quite often for Mary to manage him, which was the usual baby care stuff. Once we got there, we went in and sat down to talk with mammaw for a few minutes and unwind, as it was a long trip. James needed fed, and I needed a cup of coffee, so I went in the kitchen and made some. I sat down for a few minutes and drank my coffee, and went over to the telephone to make a call down to my ex-wife's apartment she was in at the time, and there was no answer. No answer I thought, well maybe they are in the bathroom. I kept calling and calling, and yet, there was no answer. Finally, I started calling her mother, and again, ring no answer. I was thinking to myself, what the heck, so I kept calling; a short while later, I got a call back from her mother, and she said that Leslie wasn't home. I took a short pause, a breath and sighed, and asked where Leslie was. She said that, she and Kelsey took off to go to Columbus, Ohio to her sisters for Christmas. Ok, so let me ask you something here? How is it, that I made plans, that I was entitled to, drove all the way across the state to pick up my daughter for Christmas, and her knowing I was coming, then take off to her sisters? Does that sound like she cares about Kelsey's visitation with dad to you? Does that even remotely sound like good parenting? I tell you, I was God Awful mad at that. There was no emergency, there were no major problems; but she just leaves heading to Ohio, and not a darn word to me that she was planning on leaving anyhow. She didn't even call me to let me know there was a change of plans. No Sir! She had me drive all the way 4 hours, with my son, James and Mary; just to find out they were gone. Oh Boy, I was livid, and Mary was bent out of shape over it too. I was so mad; I could have chewed a nail in two!

Not only did we take Kelsey to the zoo, I took her to a concerto in Louisville, where they perform the arts. I grew up in the country, don't get me wrong, but I am educated and cultured. She went with me, and both of us got dressed up to attend. I guess at the time, she was about 12. She looked amazing. Both of us looked like we just arrived at a Hollywood event, if that tells you the "scene" of the concerto. We found our seats and the show began.

It was the most emotional, drama of music one could ever hope to hear. There were instruments from every section of woodwind, brass, and drums. There were violinists, bass players, and every other variety of instruments you would see in an ensemble. The acoustics of the musicians was astounding, not to mention the acoustics of the building. When the music was played, it rang out and stayed out. I was really impressed with the music, however, Kelsey seemed to not enjoy it as much as I did and was telling me how bored she was. After the price I paid for us to get in there and spend some quality time together, and get some culture, I figured that she would enjoy it - I guess not.

Mary and I, or just I on occasions, would take her out to eat. She used to go out with her pappaw Bob, my father, and eat at Chinese restaurants. Kelsey took a liking to shrimp at one point and she would eat my father out of the table, which is hard, if you know how he is around the dinner table. I can't even keep up with him! We would take her out to Chinese as well, Mexican, and Italian restaurants. I am not talking the cheap kind either. These restaurants, sometimes in the 3-4 star range, would cost an arm and a leg for most people. Don't get me wrong, I wasn't rich or wealthy, but at least I had a great job at this point, and what's wrong with taking your daughter out to treat her good. There isn't any reason why I wouldn't, and besides, Mary loved the food too, and would be more than happy to go along. If you could have seen the smile on Mary's face when I told her I was going to take Kelsey out, she would say can I come along. Sure you can! It would just give us all that much more time to spend together as a family.

If I hadn't had enough worry about my daughter at this point in my life, things were starting to take a turn, at least for me. I started to see changes in my daughter's behavior. I found out some things, which I didn't approve of, as well as a lot of the things that I already hadn't approved of. Things were being hidden from me, out of an intentional lack of communication from Leslie, and I guess she had hoped I wouldn't catch on, or at least find out about what she and her husband were up to. It is amazing how when you try to keep information about your child from their other parent, it always seems to be found out, right?

Chapter 24 - The Hidden Truth

At 10 years old, my daughter Kelsey started to develop a tendency to be a 007 agent. Nothing and I mean nothing was sacred between me as a father and her as my daughter. It felt to me more than Mary, at the time, that we were under constant surveillance with her, as if she was always digging for information. We figured out, as time went on, that her mother was putting her up to these tasks to find out more of what was going on in our private lives. As time went on, we got more and more suspicious of these behaviors and felt isolated when we were around Kelsey, although I continued to be her father, and loved to try and spend time with her. Since the point my daughter was around 8, Leslie, would put Kelsey up to calling me to "speak" with me, only to have Kelsey say mom wants to talk to you about something, and hand the phone over to her. It wasn't that Kelsey actually wanted to talk with me, but that Leslie knew I was getting awfully irritated at her, and honestly, I didn't have anything to speak with her about, so she would get Kelsey to do her dirty work for her by getting me on the phone. Having a child do this for you, simply because you're too much of a coward to do it yourself, is wrong. How many of you out there would agree that having your child do this type of activity is wrong? This carried through all the way through the time she was about 12 or 13 years old, and frankly it got to the point where I didn't want to even answer the phone, because I knew my ex-wife "wanted" something. Couldn't Kelsey actually just call me, to talk with me about what I was doing, or what she needed?

Kelsey used to come to our home in Kentucky on a fairly frequent basis. During the time that I was at work during the weeks, and weekends, sometimes as a parent, caregiver, and being responsible for her as well as being responsible for all of the finances, bills, and child support to her mother, I would have to lock myself in my home office, so that I could continue to work, while she was there visiting, as well as spending time with Mary and her brother James. I guess that it upset her sometimes, because she told me many times, that I spent way too much time on the computer, but as a kid, she didn't understand the fact that it was my job, and her livelihood that it sprung from. No matter how much a parent tries to convey certain aspects of life and reality to a child, some of them simply cannot in their mind grasp the importance of our sacrifices for them. I guess expecting a child to understand may be a bit too much, but one would think that they would be grateful for what they have. There is nothing more than I wanted to do but walk out of my office, shut the darn door behind me and go out into the main part of the house, flop on the couch and snuggle that little angel of mine up, watch some TV, play some video games and relax with her. Mary was right there with us, and knew how important James and Kelsey were to me.

Working for Nuance was one of the most challenging and rewarding experiences of my life. Being a Marine, I learned all too well, the defining meaning of dedication, motivation, and being self-driven, just like many Marines before and after me. There were many weeks, because of my position I was working in excess of 70 hours a week. I was one engineer for 7 states, and all of the hospitals, clinics, and law offices that used the software suite of applications that Nuance had developed. What was my role in all of this? I was the one responsible for phone conferences, being a technical lead in the installation, architecture, testing, and systems go lives into production for these hospitals and facilities. I was also the main point of contact for the facilities in case of disaster, emergency situations, failures, or any number of other problems such as hardware failures, or technical troubleshooting. There were times that I would get emailed or called late at night, and would have to drive to remote locations 3 and 4 hours away, just to walk in and find that it was a misunderstanding from their IT staff. Then there were those times that I would have to drive all of that way to find that the system had shut down and went corrupt, and I would have hours and hours ahead of me, rebuilding and restoring these systems from the ground up, in a rush, because patient care was on the line, and in technical terms, there was a "work stoppage", for my customer. I remember being on duty so long, sometimes, that I would have sharp, head piercing pains shooting out from behind my eyes where I had been up over 72 hours at a time, driving to and from and fixing these product solutions for customers. Sometimes, because of my insane schedule for customers, the only real time that I would have time to replace parts would be in the later parts of the night, and if I was lucky, 30 minutes down the road from my office. It wasn't uncommon for me to drive out at midnight or 1 AM to take a server down for repairs. For most hospitals, a facility having the system down at all is hard to get, and when you do get the time it is always after hours.

There have even been times that, because of shortcomings in the schedules of my peer field engineers in other regions, they would ask me to fill in for them, and I would coordinate with my manager, informing him of the agreement, and I would make travel reservations. I would travel to the airport and either leave my car there, have Mary get up before the chickens started crowing and drive me, or get one of my other friends to drive me to the airport terminal. I would sometimes get there as early as 4:30 AM to get ticketed, get through airport security, and have time to walk to the terminal area before the arrival of my flight. I would get on the airplane, fly to my destination, and immediately head over to the hospital facility so that I would be able to aid the customer in resolution of their issues. When the whole of a project rests on your shoulders, and you're the buck, when the buck stops here, you take charge and lead the situation through to resolution, no matter the extra effort you have to put into it. It was rare that I would ever have to call in for backup, but there were times that I needed a second pair of eyes on a technical issue, not because I didn't know what I was doing, but because I was either so exhausted from the long travel hours, or exhausted from sitting there looking at a problem for hours on end. Sometimes, it just simply helps, to get a fresh pair of eyes on a problem to see what the root cause is, whereas if I was rested I would have most likely seen it. Sometimes I would simply call to get verification, and talk through the problem with another peer engineer, just to make sure that I was correct in my analysis and to see if there was another possible fix that I could use that might be better than what I was going to do in order to fix any given problem.

I used to get together with Mary, James, and Kelsey and go out running the roads, just to spend time together. What I used to think was the funniest thing in the world is going out with sissy to Mexican restaurants. Some of the entrees you get at these restaurants come out on a huge plate, even for an adult. Do you know the old expression, "You've bit off more than you can chew", well that was what was so darn funny to me. Here sits this petite little blonde, and out comes the waiter, with a serving plate twice as big as she was. She would just look down at the plate, and her eyes would get so huge, because she knew there was no way, on earth, that she was going to be able to eat even a small portion of the food that was just sat in front of her. Yea, I know, it was a waste of food for the most part, but the experience for her and I was that of humor, and fun, and I really loved seeing her with that surprised look on her face.

The hardest part of spending time with Kelsey was always coordinating with her, in order to come and pick her up. I know, there was this little thing called the divorce decree and child visitation order, but I always tried to keep in mind her schedule with her mother, and if she had something important going on, I always tried to respect that, instead of demanding that Leslie have her ready for pickup. I tried to always be reasonable, but Leslie would, in a second, disagree saying that I was not reasonable, and I was not easy to get along with. I guess since 99% of the hundreds of people that I deal with on a daily basis I get along with, you will have to make your own determination as to whether I was reasonable or not. What drove me crazy was when I would call down to speak with my daughter at her mother's. I learned that Leslie or her husband Gerald would get on the other line quietly and listen to our conversations. I didn't know about this for the longest time, but it was an outright violation of ethics and privacy between me and my daughter, not that I had anything to hide, but still. Would you feel violated if that ever happened to you? This wasn't just an isolated situation either; it was an ongoing problem that happened each and every time that I would call to speak with Kelsey. The older Kelsey got, the worse it got. I am not sure what on earth crawled on my ex-wife, but it was disrespectful, and simply uncalled for behavior that reasonable people would not consider normal behavior. I just simply have to ask you one thing. What type of person would do that? For that matter, my father has had this to say about the situation as well!

"Leslie has been a pain in the rear to all of us. She used to call constantly complaining about Cleland. I can imagine what she was telling Kelsey about her dad. She married a guy that doesn't like work and wants Cleland to provide for all of them. She complains that Cleland gets to take vacations. She complains that Cleland has a newer car. She wants what Cleland has but she nor the new husband wants to work for it."

Bob James

Chapter 25 - Can You Believe the Nerve?

It was now 2010, and I was still working for Nuance. I was still running full bore with the company, heading up projects, making sure customers were taken care of and traveling all over my region, and as well, out in the western part of the United States as well as Georgia, and sometimes Mississippi. I will be honest, I was strung out from the constant travel, multiple simultaneous projects and being away from Mary, and James, and Kelsey. I didn't get to spend nearly as much time as I wanted to with these important people in my life, because my job was calling me away, and I was the only one in my area who could and would handle these projects to the best of my God given talent and abilities. At the time, Kelsey was now 12 years old and starting to develop a talkative relationship with Mary. She was starting to understand that daddy was a busy man and had a lot going on but was still upset with me because I couldn't always be there. I still felt it important however that she spend time with Mary and her brother, as they were also an integral part of her life.

At the time, I just so happened to be in Mississippi on assignment. I remember that Mary was at our home and Kelsey was there helping her, in for her visit. It was after I got back from assignment, that Mary had told me that Kelsey was helping her rearrange our kitchen pantry, because it was a disaster. You know how things get when you're constantly on the go, cooking for the family and in and out of the house with kids. Anyone who has kids or knows someone with kids has a good idea of the mess that can build up, even in the smallest of places. James was about 3 years old at the time, and frankly I don't know how Mary managed to juggle the tasks, but if you knew her, you would realize how amazing of a woman she really is. She is a homemaker, and can cook some of the most amazing dishes you would ever care to put your lips on. She gets involved with my projects, and when I ask her to do anything, she will take care of it, except the coffee. For some reason, when I ask for coffee, it rarely gets made. I don't know, maybe it's a foreign language, and she doesn't understand what Folgers is. No seriously, she really compliments me, because where I can't keep up, she does it for me.

Much much later, as a matter of fact, more than 6 months later, Mary and I were sitting in the living room, and I was having my coffee, and she and I were watching some TV trying to relax. Mary was talking to me about some of our finances, and what was going on at the Masonic Lodge, and somehow Kelsey came into the conversation. I can't remember the exact specifics, but we were talking about all of my trips that I had made with Nuance, and laughing about some of my "mishaps" during my travels. My previous trip to Mississippi, mentioned earlier, came up and I had told Mary that I was so hungry when I landed, that I skipped dropping off my baggage at the hotel I had reservations at and went straight over to the seafood restaurant where they had an, all you can eat, catfish buffet. I have to tell you, I love catfish. During the course of that conversation, Mary was telling me again about the time that Kelsey was helping her organize the pantry, and hadn't really "disclosed" everything to me before, because she didn't want to hurt my feelings or upset me. I was thinking to myself, what could be so bad, right? Well, Mary told me that Kelsey came right out and said, "I think of Gerald as more of a dad than Cleland". Now, how is it, that I provide, and make sure Kelsey has ever last thing she could possibly need, spend time with her, make sure she gets to Florida to see her mammaw and pappaw, and all at the same time hold down a job that should take 10 people to do? What on earth do you mean that you "think" of him as more of a dad than me? How could you possibly look at this guy as a father? He sits home, complaining of medical problems that don't exist, as an excuse to not hold a job, and then on top of that, does car repos on the side, with only a high school diploma and no college degree or formal training.

During the latter part of the year, during the winter of 2010, I had vacation planned for the family. I had this vacation time planned off, 2 months in advance, along with my reservations at my resort accommodations in Virginia. The whole reason why I scheduled the vacation was so that I could get away from work a little while and spend time with my family, along with the fact I wanted to have Kelsey go along with us, so it would be Mary, Kelsey and I. The destination was an educational outing for all of us. Now, I had been there a few times in the past, but Mary, and certainly not Kelsey had been there before, and that is Colonial Williamsburg. For those of you who have not had the pleasure of going there before, I really suggest it. It is an old Colonial Settlement, and they dress, act, and live just like you would in the Colonial settlements. It is highly interactive with the public, and you get to see and be a part of the life that the colonists lived. It is one of the most extraordinary things you could do on vacation. Mary and I drove over to Eastern Kentucky to pick Kelsey up, and stopped by my grandmother's home to call ahead to let them know we were close. Now, well in advance, my ex-wife knew that we were coming to get Kelsey for the vacation, however, once we got there, she refused to let Kelsey go, because there was supposed to be snow. Mary and I ended up going on the vacation without Kelsey because of that, but guess what, it didn't snow the entire time we were gone, not one flake. Kelsey missed out on an adventure, because her mother wouldn't let me take her for the trip.

Prearranged Absence Request

Prearranged absences will **NOT** be authorized during state testing
Prearranged absences will **NOT** be authorized during High School Exams

If the pre-arranged absence is for a college visit, you must also complete a College Visit Confirmation form.

Student _____ Grade __6th__

Date(s) of planned absences   18-26 December

Date student will return to school 27-December

Reasons for absence   Family Christmas Vacation

By signing below, I verify that I am the parent/ legal guardian of the above named student, and plan to remove my child from the formal academic program at ____ McKell Middle ____ School during the dates noted. (This form is not required for Dr. appt.'s etc.)

I acknowledge the Greenup County School District policy for prearranged absences and that my child's teachers are not expected to tutor my child for work missed. This request to excuse my child is made **AT LEAST ONE WEEK PRIOR** to the first day of the planned absence. Make up of assignments given during an unexcused absence will follow Board of Education Policy. My child is responsible for obtaining assignments from each teacher before the absence.

I further acknowledge that any assignment given during the absence period will be due within the school/district time frame for make up work. Any assignment that is not submitted at that time will be scored as a grade of 0%. Any tests missed will be made up within a reasonable time frame, as determined by the teachers.

Teachers Signatures: (Must be obtained at least one week in advance and prior to administrative approval)

1ST Period _____   4TH Period _____

2ND Period _____   5TH Period _____

3RD Period _____   6TH Period _____

Parent / Guardian _____   DATE _____ 2010

Principal _____   DATE _____

There was a point in time that they were using a tow truck to go get car repossessions, which requires a certain level of strength. I am sorry, but that sickens me! Sometime around this time is when I found out that my ex-wife and her husband were taking my daughter out on car repos. Having a background in police work, I knew that the job contained an element of danger that a child should not be exposed to. I had a conversation with my ex-wife in regards to this and told her that I did not feel comfortable nor did I want her to take my daughter out on car repos anymore. Her reasoning for doing so was that if the party saw a child in the vehicle that they would be less likely to be aggressive. I told her that there is a high possibility that she was going to go repo a vehicle from somebody and that they were going to step outside with a gun and start shooting. I asked her if having a child in the vehicle is going to stop a 12 gauge slug. In my mind, and other reasonable people's minds, putting a child in harm's way in a profession such as car repos, is not acceptable nor is it safe. Wouldn't you agree with that? Even after that conversation the trips on car repos did not stop, and my ex-wife continued to take my daughter with her, without my permission and this continues even today. My daughter seems to have this expectation in her mind that it is fun, driving down the road fast, windows down, radio blasting, with not a care in the world, but little does she know the danger that she is in.

I work extremely hard for what I get, and that is the gratitude that my daughter, Kelsey, has to give me? If that were me, I would find every way possible to work, because I cannot sit idly by, and not be doing something productive. Really? I think there is something really wrong with that, don't you? Even, however, after being insulted to no reproach, Leslie would still, from time to time, call me up and tell me that she needed money for Kelsey's school supplies, or school pictures, or clothes. Now keep in mind, that my mother and father would come up and buy her a boatload of clothes during the year to do her, and also shoes. There was even one time that my mother and father bought her an entire bedroom set, chest of drawers, bed, nightstand, and desk, so she would have some place to do her homework in the quiet of her room. They never asked me if they could, but they were right in their assumption, that I wouldn't mind them helping her. There were times that Leslie would come to me, and I would give her extra money, and I would tell her not to let Kelsey know it came from me. I wanted Kelsey to think good of her mother, but I also wanted her to think good of me as well. One such example came about when she called me asking for a few hundred dollars for a trampoline, and I obliged, since it was an investment for my daughter.

Chapter 26 - Forensic Technical Recon

Just like every other child on the planet, they think that their parents are stupid, and don't know anything, or don't know what to look for. Unluckily for my daughter, my extensive computer and technical background provides the knowledge set that I need to keep an eye on my daughter. I would have seriously not been paying attention in school, to obtain the positions that I have reached during my lifetime, otherwise I would be working at a fast food restaurant.   No offense to anybody out there who does work at fast food restaurants, but I chose a different path, which deals with a lot of school and a lot of knowledge, which is something a lot of people don't want to invest the time to do.

While continuing my research, keeping an eye on my daughter, I found her on an adult dating website, at 12 years old, looking for older guys. I took a printout of my findings and filed those aside, at which point I called the customer service number on the website's "about us" page buried way down deep. I explained to them who I was, and why I was calling, and asked them if they monitored their website for underage children.   I went on to explain to them that I had found my daughter's profile on their website, and that she was clearly a minor. They said that this does happen sometimes, and that they take the profiles down at request, once notified. They made good on their word and immediately took the profile down, but not before I got the printout for evidence. I then called my ex-wife, and asked her about the profile. She said that she did not know anything about it - what a magical surprise. Nothing really surprises me, especially when it's coming from the attention of my ex-wife watching my daughter. My ex-wife's ability to monitor my child is, in all intents and purposes, non-existent. Over the course of the years, there have been multiple times that I have gone to her with information which I had managed to locate electronically about Kelsey, and she was completely clueless about any of it. How could you be living in the same house with your child, and not know? Really? Lord knows that with my children being in my house, I would know every move they made, and could sniff out any suspicious activity faster than a Blue Heeler hound.

Upon one visit to my ex-wife's house to pick up and drop off my daughter, Leslie and Gerald approached me as they had found that Kelsey had created an account for email on Yahoo's website. She had to have a way, email wise, to register on these websites. I had a strict rule at the time, that I didn't want my teenage daughter, just making herself at home, on the internet without supervision. It was unfortunate for me that I could not personally supervise her, but rather my ex-wife and her husband Gerald. Neither of them knew much about technology, so when it came to "sneaking" behind her mother's back she started to become a professional. At the request of my ex-wife, I got on their computer and attempted recovery of her email address on Yahoo that they had located. After extensive research on the computer I was unable to personally recover her password. I told my ex-wife that I wanted to speak with my daughter, in their office, to get a resolution to this problem. We brought Kelsey in and sat her down behind the computer, and explained to her the extent of the trouble that she was in for lying to us. I asked her to unlock her yahoo account, and Kelsey pretended that she didn't know what we were talking about, and pretended that she didn't know what the password was so we never got into the account. I have a feeling that there was more information in that account than what Kelsey was acting like. I even went to the extent of having my attorney's office send a letter to one of our Law Firms in the state of California to gain access to her account. Neither that nor the attempt to contact Yahoo directly yielded any results. Even though her mother and I had joint legal custody over her, as our child, we had no legal rights, over their policies; to access her email account therefore they would not grant access. Doesn't this sound like a clear violation of parental rights to you? Apparently Yahoo policy outweighs law! I know this sounds ridiculous, but it is what I have found out from experience dealing with this. My suggestion to you parents, who want to keep an eye on their children, is to install some surveillance software on your computer if you're going to let your child use the computer for any amount of time privately, or for that matter, confiscate their smartphone, and install surveillance software on it as well. It isn't that we "don't trust" our children, but rather we have to be proactive and smarter than they are. This is just a small example of the difference between education, and not being educated. As a technical engineer in my field, I know how to monitor a child's usage on a computer without them knowing, so that I can keep reins on what they are doing without me being there. If they're going to websites that they should not be going to, I would know pretty much immediately.

Chapter 27 - A Loan - What is that?

Banks here, banks there, banks everywhere. This is where you go to get loans of every shape and size tailored to the person asking. You need a loan for a house? You go see your banker. What about consolidation loans for bills? Your banker can help you out with that as well. Not satisfied with their interest rate? In today's society you can simply go to Google, type in what you're looking for, and get an answer. Google has become one of the world's most renowned search engines for just about anything that you could possibly want. If you wanted to compare loan rates for example, you would simply type that into Google and find a web page that can give you comparative rates for loans, and then you can decide whether or not the interest rate fits your budget, but this isn't a book about financing, nor is it a book about banks. It is a book with what on earth happened to my kid!

Let me paint you a picture for a moment. Some people decide that they want an education, whereas other people decide that they didn't want an education. Remember earlier, when I told you, how important education was to my family? The people who decided that they want to be prepared for life, did, go on to higher education, and went out into the job market to find a career job. The ones who decided to not pursue their higher education, ended up with a normal job, which is not a career. Do you know the difference in the two? Some don't!

For example, you go out and decide that you're going to buy a McDonald's franchise. That would be a career based move, as an asset, and a business opportunity an educated and financial based decision. Most likely if you buy a McDonald's franchise, you've probably got other real estate as well, bringing in additional revenue. A lot of investment companies out there buy up businesses, which generate revenue to their bottom line. If they make an educated purchase, and the business doesn't pan out, most of the time, they will get resold, as they went from being an asset to a liability. I suggest looking the definitions of these two up, so you can be clear on what I am talking about, if you are not sure. You may also be a vice president of a bank, or a high level executive at a real estate agency. These are examples of career based jobs. Other career based jobs might include managing a telecommunications company, or having a position as a director in a division of a company. These positions are hard to come by, and only go to the most educated people, whom have degrees, usually in management.

Those people who decided to not further their education, most likely have a regular job, and most of them hate it. How many people do you know, on a daily basis, complain that they are having problems making ends meet, or they wish, later in life, that they went on to college? These types of decisions only lead to problems and stress later in life. I say, be prepared, just like the "Boy Scout" motto. Examples to these types of jobs, would be fast food restaurants, department store employees, teenage jobs such as working at amusement parks, car washes, pizza delivery, and other local businesses which pay minimum wage or a little higher. These types of jobs are not considered career positions, and are not designed to make a living at. They are designed, so that a person going to school can provide a living for themselves, or at least "get by" until they get their degree and move forward in their life. A career job, in today's society, usually offers a 401k retirement plan, stock in the company, and health benefit plans, such as medical, dental, and vision. Some companies even now days are offering flexible spending accounts for your medical expenses, whereas the company automatically takes money out of your paycheck, and you use that money solely for medical expenses, such as deductibles and medications. Would you get those types of benefits working as a cashier at a department store, or a stock clerk at a gas station? Would you get those types of benefits working at a gas station as an attendant? I further ask you, would you expect to get those types of benefits driving pizza for a local restaurant to someone's home?

Something, somewhere, has seriously gone wrong with the expectations of our citizens in the United States, whereas people seem to expect the same things as those who have worked hard all of their life to achieve. Some people believe that they are entitled to be able to drive nice vehicles, go out to eat any time that they want to, go on vacation, and not have to work for that which they want. Does that even remotely sound right to you in your mind? Do you as a hard working person feel that you should foot the bill for somebody who does not want to put forth the effort of self-improvement? Of course you wouldn't have any problem helping your children, but what about everybody else in the United States? I am not one of those people who feel that I should foot the bill for someone who does not put forth the effort to better themselves in society. Don't get me wrong, there are those types of people who literally do need assistance, because either they are not able to fend for themselves due to severe medical problems or have run into a situation in life as to where they actually do need assistance. I don't mind to help those types of people. God knows, in my life, there were times that I worked my butt off, and was doing great, then flopped right on my face. Yes, in those times, I reached out to those with the ability to assist me, but only in my mind, with full intentions of repaying my debts. Which leads me to my point, what is a loan? A loan is a simple promise to pay the money back with interest.

Chapter 28 - The Birth of Deception

It was about this point in time, during the summer of 2011, when Kelsey was about 13 years old, I received a call from my ex-wife Leslie, asking me one of the most hilarious and ridiculous question that she could possibly come to me with. She kept calling and calling, but I was downright busy, sitting in my office, on the phone with customers, so I couldn't break free to get her call. Finally, I yelled out in the living room, and said, "Mary, can you get the phone the next time Leslie calls and find out what she wants." Mary answered the phone, and asked Leslie what she could help her out with, and she said that she would prefer to wait and talk with Cleland about it. After a few minutes, she told Mary what she wanted, and Mary brought the phone to me in the office. I had to ask my customer if I could call them back in a few minutes, and hung up the phone, so I could take the "all important" phone call from my ex-wife. She said and I quote, "Can I get a car loan of $3000 from you so I can buy a car."

Now after all of the past problems I received from my ex-wife, all of the trouble she had given me in picking up my daughter Kelsey, all of the invasion of privacy on the phone, the fact that she was cheating on me, and left me for her husband, the requests for money to "help" her out along the way, and her lack of follow through with going to get her GED, and head to college, I couldn't help but to laugh. That's right, I laughed right in her face, HA! Why? In my mind, that was one of the most asinine questions that she could come to me with. I could swear, at that exact moment, I was sitting in an episode of "Jerry Seinfeld", where Kramer would come barging into Jerry's apartment asking him some crazy question with his hair all spiked up. My response to her was, "Get your husband to get you a loan at the bank." Why in the world, after all that she had put me, and my family through, up to this point, would I ever in a million years consider doing such a thing? It would be a bad business decision, and a capital liability, which I knew would never get repaid. She didn't have any credit, her husband didn't have any credit, and I knew she didn't have any credit. Why else would she come to me asking me such a moronic question? Not to mention, like I said earlier about education, and the "wants" of those who don't have one. Better luck next time I say!

Somewhere about this time, I found out through Kelsey that she had been shooting guns. Now I don't have any problem with shooting guns, but I had a major problem in how it was done. First off, I am well trained in the use of firearms. As a Marine, I learned how to maintenance and secure every weapon that you could carry or shoot. I learned firearms safety, wind control, zeroing of your weapons, and could shoot at a mile accurately with very little deviation. Secondly, as a Military Police officer, I was also trained to shoot, and was required to shoot for qualification, accuracy and safety. What I am telling you is this, I am well trained and know how to teach my child how to shoot, when the time was ready, but I didn't feel like she was ready, therefore, I didn't start teaching her yet. Through Kelsey, I found out that Gerald has been teaching my daughter to shoot. Good God! If I wanted an ignorant, untrained gunslinger to teach my daughter, I would have sent her out to the big city to find a gang to join up with. NO! I didn't agree with my ex-wife allowing this, and I had multiple talks with her. It is a father's job to teach their child, and it's really clear that Gerald is not her father. He is just a sit in, that isn't qualified, nor trained in firearms or safety. How much, as a father, am I supposed to keep my mouth shut, so I don't upset anyone. I am done with keeping my mouth shut! What say you about that? Oh yes, I want the world to know of my sacrifice, my trials, and my experience dealing with these issues, as I am sure I am not the only one that feels this way.

Right about the beginning of the year in 2011, James was admitted to the hospital in Louisville, Kentucky. The poor little guy was only four years old, and his eye had swollen shut due to an upper respiratory infection and sinus blockage. I really felt bad for James, because of his age, and that he could not see out of one eye. It was during this time, I was still working for my company putting in excessive hours; but I did not take off of work nor did I leave James alone. I took my laptop and the books that I needed, and set up an office inside of his hospital room. It was from that room that I worked for nearly 2 weeks, and watched over my son in the process while Mary was back at the house resting. She would come up every day to visit for a few hours, traveling back and forth between there and the house and would stay until the evening. The nurses were kind enough to loan me a plastic wagon from the kids' center, and I would pull James around the hospital in that, just to get him out of his hospital room for a little while. Could you imagine a four-year-old, in a hospital bed, with one eye swollen shut, and IVs running into his arm? It was hard enough to get him to sit still for five minutes at the house, let alone two weeks in a hospital bed.

Around this time, my father decided to buy Kelsey a small ASUS laptop for her to keep in touch with me and her grandparents in Florida. My father set the laptop up with remote control tools, so that I could manage her laptop, and so I could keep an eye on her to make sure she wasn't using the laptop at her age for things she shouldn't be watching, or listening to. Periodically I would jump on her laptop to update software or to uninstall something, manage malware, or other aspects of computer maintenance. On one specific day I wanted to check out what my daughter was doing, and I remoted into the machine. I was greeted by my daughter, yelling at me through the chat program demanding I get off her laptop. I said, "Look here missy, let go of the keyboard and mouse," so I could check on the computer. Instead of her doing just that, she started typing, and moving the mouse intentionally to keep me from doing what I needed to do. In short terms, it really made me mad. I called down to her mother's house at the time and Leslie answered the phone. I demanded that she put Kelsey on the phone with me, because of what she was doing. She wouldn't let me speak with her because I was mad. After several attempts to speak with her, I finally hung up the phone. You are right, I was mad, and I had a right to be with my child acting out. My responsibility was to ensure my daughter wasn't watching, seeing, or hearing anything out of the age group she was in, and I planned on making sure that was not going to happen. Leslie stated to me, "I don't want you upsetting Kelsey and you're not going to talk to her if you're mad." Excuse me, but what reasonable minded person would be worried as a parent to set their child straight, mad or not? It was point blank wrong for my ex-wife to keep me from doing my job, and as you can clearly tell throughout this text, it's not the first or the last time that it happened.

In May of 2011, my daughter Michelle was born. Boy was I happy, because I had a daughter who, despite all of the drama, I could cuddle up, love, spend time with, have a sibling for James, and who would actually be there for him. She was just amazing when she was born. She came out with red hair, and these bright eyes. Although there was a high level of stress associated with bringing a new child into the world, there was also the joy of being a father to a new baby girl. Yes, I will admit I was overwhelmed; but it was in a good way, and I certainly was ready for the little thing.

When Mary got pregnant with Katie, it was a shocker for both of us, and even today, it is hard to believe that she is here with us.

As I had previously mentioned, my family stressed a high importance on education, and the Marine Corps stressed a high importance on setting the example. I wanted my daughter to have a good example, for her future education; therefore, my intention was to help set the stage for that example. On three separate occasions I went to the local community college, and obtained a register of classes, and the information about child care at the institution. For students, they offer free childcare, at the daycare in the lower level of the institution. This is to allow convenience for the parents who are trying to further their education. On these three separate occasions, I hand delivered the registrar of classes, the financial aid paperwork, and a hint of hope that my ex-wife would be the one to set the example for our daughter, in her household. I, myself, am a highly educated person, because I have pushed myself to that point and I had the support of my father and mother behind me to get the job done. It is important to have a good example set for you, for your life as a child, and future. In all of the times that I had delivered this information, my ex-wife decided to ignore and not pursue the path that I had set before her. If you'll remember the old adage, "you can lead a horse to water, but you can't make it drink," that was my ex-wife in this example. I tried to help, but that was the best that I could do, as it was a decision, that my ex-wife choose to stay in the situation that she was in. I specifically remember being on the phone with Leslie at the time, and she said and I quote," Why is it so important to you that I go to college?" I laughed and said, "Is this a rhetorical question?", as if my logic didn't make any sense whatsoever to her. Apparently the common sense factor didn't dawn on her, yet another amazing surprise for me!

Apparently attention isn't one of those things that makes sense to some people. How can people go day to day and not notice the simple things around them? I don't know, but there are times that I wonder how these same people even manage to put their pants on in the mornings, and find the door to get outside. I am sure you know some people like that, and I am sure that you have wondered the same thing. I can't remember the exact dates, but I do know that this event happened during the year, sometime, when Kelsey was 13 years old. I had been communicating with my ex-wife and her husband Gerald, because I was continually trying to develop some type of relationship with them, to make life easier on Kelsey. It was told to me by Gerald that he was at home one day, with Kelsey, and Leslie was gone somewhere at the time. Priscilla was there as well, and was back in Kelsey's bedroom at their home. Gerald had not seen Kelsey for some time, so he went back to her bedroom to check on her and the door was barricaded. He shoved the door open, and low and behold, there sits Priscilla on the computer in Kelsey's room, stripping on webcam for someone, while my daughter Kelsey and Priscilla's daughter were in the room. Both of the kids were 13 years old at the time, and he ripped her butt and threw her out of the house. Now, there are a lot of things that I did not agree with; but that was one decision I stood behind. Having exposed my child to that type of behavior, she should have been arrested and thrown in the clink. It was hard to tell what on earth was on the screen of that laptop, and for how long, while our 13 year olds were in that room with her. I told Leslie that I never want that lady around my daughter again, and for good reason. She said that she wasn't allowed back over to her house. Not more than 2 weeks later, Priscilla was back over there hanging around again. Leslie justified it as Priscilla was going through a hard breakup with her boyfriend, and that they were friends. Really? So that makes it ok?

Around the beginning of the year in 2012, Mary had her back go out on her and she was bed ridden. She, at first was having pains in her back; but it worsened to the point of having an ambulance come to the house to get her to take her to the hospital. Mary ended up being admitted to the hospital in Louisville. Not only was her back messed up, she had a urinary tract infection, a busted eardrum, and her white blood cell count was through the roof. The hospital staff ended up putting a tube in her ear, administering medications via IV, and keeping her under constant observation. Because of the elevated white blood cell count, they called in a infectious disease doctor, a neurologist for her back, and an Otolaryngologist (ENT) for her ear problem. She stayed in the hospital for 2 weeks, and I visited her on a regular basis with the kids, but was also holding down my job with Nuance at the same time at my home office, so you could imagine the stress I was under taking care of a 7 month old daughter and a 4 year old son. I called and spoke with my mother in Florida, and she made plans to come up and help me take care of Mary and the kids. Mom flew in from Florida, and I went to the airport in Louisville to pick her up. We went back to the house to let my mother get settled in, and sometime between then and shortly after, I brought Mary back to the house. Since mammaw was in, she also wanted to see Kelsey so I went over to Eastern Kentucky, to bring her back for the weekend.

Mom stayed for a couple of months until April of 2012, to help out, and it was very much appreciated, as it was chaotic to render medical aid, and work at the same time.

I was very active in the Masonic Lodge at the time with other Freemasons, and my friends Johnny, who was my age, and Levi, one of the older members who came over to the house for frequent visits, as I to their houses. One of the nights, prior to us bedding down, Kelsey went into the bathroom to get her night clothes on, and came out. She threw her skinny jeans pants over in front of the dog kennel in the living room. Mom, Mary, and I told her that she had better move her pants, because of the dog. Apparently, she didn't listen to any of us, so the next morning when we got up, the exact same pair of "favorite" skinny jeans were torn to shreds by my dog Beau. Let me be the one to tell you, it was "drama." Kelsey was throwing a complete fit, because the dog ate her jeans. I said to Kelsey, "I warned you about the dog and what would happen if you didn't put your jeans up." I mean "really", what did she want me to say? I could have moved the pants myself, but it was a lesson to be learned for her, since she decided that she wasn't going to listen to 3 grown adults. I called up my friend Johnny from the lodge and asked him if he wanted to make a run with me, so Kelsey and I got in my car, drove over to get him, and proceeded to the "nearest" Old Navy Outlet, to get a replacement pair of jeans for Kelsey, which was 3 ½ hours North to Dayton, Ohio. That is correct, you heard me right, I drove her that far to get a simple pair of jeans, because I couldn't listen to the drama any more, and neither could mom or Mary. It would have been nice, if she would have picked her pants up to begin with, but that didn't pan out.

It was a long drive up to Dayton that day, but it was nice weather, and it gave me and Johnny some time to talk about events at the Lodge, and it also gave Kelsey and I time to talk as well. Although it was because of "drama" that we were out to begin with, it was actually an enjoyable outing to see some scenery, and Kelsey had not been to Dayton, Ohio, before; so it was another opportunity for her to get out of the country, and into the big city so she would understand that life wasn't all trees and dogs. Granted, I grew up in the country, but after I got out of the house, I learned that there was a much bigger world than what I had seen before. Once we finally arrived at the mall area in Dayton, Johnny, Kelsey, and I went into the Old Navy store and proceeded to find the jeans that would replace the ones my dog "Beau" ate. We shopped for hours, and Kelsey tried on several pairs of jeans. She also tried on shoes, shirts, and many other articles of clothing. We were there for a while, but honestly I didn't mind, because at least she could get a replacement pair of jeans, and I needed to get out of the house for a little while anyhow. At one of the many stores we went in, Kelsey needed to try on some shirts, and of course daddy helped carry the load of laundry back to the dressing room. Johnny, who was looking at some clothes himself, was maybe 10 feet or less from where I was standing outside of the dressing room waiting on Kelsey to come out and show me her outfit. Here she comes rounding the corner, and walks right up to me, boobs hanging out of her shirt. I said, "Sis, put those darn things away," and Johnny just happened to see what I was yelling about, and turned blood red and turned around. Kelsey just shrugged her shoulders and said, "I don't care". I told her to walk back into that dressing room, and put something on that wasn't revealing and was respectable. I certainly wasn't going to let her get clothing like that, and although I wanted her to get clothing, it had better be respectful clothes. Once we were done getting her pair of jeans, she had also accumulated another $300 in clothes. I didn't really mind, because she needed some clothes.

Not too long after Kelsey, Johnny, and I got back to the house in Kentucky, her temperature went through the roof and it was all I could do to hold her temperature down. Let's just put it this way, it was a really long evening and night. I put Kelsey in a lukewarm bath to reduce temperature, administered liquid Ibuprofen and Tylenol alternating every 4 hours, with cool cloths to reduce the core temperature. The poor little thing was delusional, and after a short bit of time in the bathtub, she was able to sleep, because her temperature came down to a point where she was able to rest. It was any wonder that I was able to get any work done, but it was a challenging time none-the-less. Mary was unable to help me, because she literally couldn't move, and she was in the bed. Any slight movement of her back, and she was moaning in pain. Mom couldn't help me either at that point because sometime during the middle part of her visit, she came down really ill herself with a bronchial infection that put her in bed as well. It was again, much more difficult for me to work, and maintain my position with Nuance. At this point, I could not travel much to do my job, so I was doing much of my work remotely, with the exception of local travel to Louisville. Most of my outings involved trips back and forth to the pharmacy.

Sometime shortly after, I believe it may have been the next weekend, I drove over from Shelbyville to see Kelsey. She wanted to go horseback riding. No One in my family, except my uncle had horses, but he rarely rode them, so I had to find another place for her to ride. I must have stayed on Google for 4 hours on my phone, and visited at least 5 places, but finally I was able to locate a stables in Carter County Kentucky. We were out for a long time, just to find a horse for Kelsey to ride. We finally arrived at our destination, and Kelsey didn't have much experience with horses like I did, so I helped her get saddled up, and I rode with her as well as the instructor. For each ride, 3 total, it costed me $38 dollars at a total cost of $114, just to ride. I thought Kelsey and I had a pretty good time. After we were done with that, we decided to visit my uncle's farm, where the log cabin my family built still stands. My mammaw and pappaw used to go out there a lot, so there is a lot of memories surrounding that cabin. I wanted to take Kelsey out there, so we could rough it for the weekend. I stopped and bought a bunch of supplies, food, pack, cooking utensils, and everything else that we would need for the weekend. We drove up, got the keys off of my uncle and Kelsey and I drove down the hill, so that we could check the cabin for bugs and animals.

I opened the door to the cabin and peeked in, and there were spiders everywhere. I backed out of the cabin and ran back to the local department store so that I could get some spray of all kinds. I wasn't planning on going to sleep unless I could be sure Kelsey and I weren't going to get eat up by insects. I went back and sprayed upstairs and downstairs. I literally hosed the walls of the log cabin down with Raid. While I was inside taking care of this, Kelsey was standing outside next to my vehicle waiting on me. On my way up the stairs to the top loft, I caught a twinkle of reflection in my eye. I turned my head slow, as I was already on guard, and there, 2 inches from my nose on the top rail of the ceiling was a 30 inch copperhead stake coiled up asleep. I started bleeding sweat beads down my forehead, and slowly backed down the stairs, keeping my eye on that nuisance. I made it out the door without the snake catching on to what was going on, since I was being quiet. Kelsey asked me, "What is wrong?" I told her, and again, we went up to my uncles and I spoke with him about it. He said that the best thing I could do is use a wasp spray that shoots long distance foam and he happened to have a can out in the garage. Kelsey and I drove back down again to deal with this problem. Kelsey stayed outside next to the car with the door open as I told her copperhead snakes are ferocious and will chase you. I wanted a safe haven in my car in case it decided to chase me! I walked in, zeroed in on its eyes, and nailed it square the first attempt. I kept the trigger down on the spray can for at least 3 seconds and sure enough it came slithering down the roof chasing me. It was moving fast too, and I yelled at Kelsey while I was running out the door, as if my tail was on fire, and told her to jump in. I did the same thing and waited to see if the snake would come out. After about 5 minutes, that snake still hadn't come out the door. I was afraid to walk back in there, because there was a chance that it was laying on the inside wall next to the door. Kelsey and I abandoned our idea of staying in the cabin and stayed the night at my uncle's house instead.

In Mid-May of 2012 I paid $314.00 for airplane tickets to fly Kelsey to Florida for the summer, to spend some time with her mammaw and pappaw who lived there. My father had taken her to Kennedy Space center and a few other places, including on a hovercraft on Alligator Alley. By the time the beginning of June rolled around, she was throwing a complete fit on mom and dad wanting to go home. It was so bad in fact, that my mother called me begging me to let her take my daughter home. As a result of this, mom had to drive 17 hours on a seconds notice to take her back to Kentucky. I was really upset with Kelsey. I had done told her, before I spent all of that money, that I expected her to spend the whole summer school break with her mammaw and pappaw. I told her, under no uncertain terms, that she needed to sit her butt down, apologize to her grandparents for giving them a hard time, and forget coming back to her mother's till summer was over, since she made a commitment. A child has to learn their responsibility somehow, right? My mother and father, against my better thought, did what they had to do and drove her home.

Between June and November of 2012, Kelsey was on another mad streak at me and wouldn't talk to me for weeks even if I would call or get on the computer to talk to her, from where I had to talk direct to her, because of her behavior at her mammaw's home in Florida. I sent her flowers to say "I am sorry" for having to get on you, but I was trying to do my job. After a week or two passed, I never got a letter, phone call, email, or nothing from Kelsey to thank me for the flowers. I got tired of waiting and called my ex-wife to speak with her about the situation. She said that Kelsey didn't want to talk to me, and that she told her that she needed to call me to say thank you, which never happened. I confronted my ex-wife about the issue and told her that she could have called me and handed the phone to Kelsey, however, she stated, "That is child abuse." Is that really child abuse, or just bad parenting?

During the course of Kelsey's visit to Florida, my father bought her an IPAD to play with. I didn't really want her to have one, because of all of the behavioral problems; but he did because he wanted her to have something nice. After 2 weeks, once Kelsey made it home, she dropped it and cracked the screen on it. From that point, Gerald started using the IPAD to take pictures of VIN numbers, as well as TAG numbers of vehicles he was repossessing. This information was emailed via the email account which my father set up for Kelsey, so it is my dad's email account. The pictures are still stored there electronically. Since I found they were abusing the account that was setup for my daughter, I changed the password and locked them out. The emails as well as the pictures are still located there.

Chapter 29 - A New School?

Now, during the latter part of the school year, while my daughter was still in middle school, she was starting to develop some bad habits and was hanging around the wrong kids. I did not want my daughter hanging around bad influences, nor did I want her developing habits that she was learning from these kids. As a result to her behavior, her mother and I had spoken and decided that we were going to get her out of public, mainstream school, while the time was still ok. We took her to a private Christian school in Eastern Kentucky close to where my ex-wife lived, and had her evaluated. Kelsey seemed to like the idea of the school, as it had basketball, volleyball, and a gymnasium as well. I know that I really liked it, because the students had a dress code, everyone was equal, there were smaller classrooms, and it would give Kelsey a chance to raise her grades fast. There were even tutors who would work with the students' one on one who were having problems in subjects. Now granted, after the evaluation test Kelsey took, they were going to hold her a year behind, they stated that they would be able to catch her up throughout the year and move her ahead to the grade that she was supposed to be in. They were willing to do whatever we needed them to in order to help our daughter get more attention on her education, and at the same time, separate her from the bad aspects of the school that she was going to. I was really excited for my daughter, and I called up the uniform shop, in Ohio, who made their school uniforms and put hers on order to be made, and paid for them up front. They had to make a trip to the school anyhow that week, so they were happy to deliver them over there at no charge to me, so I was really happy.

As part of our agreement to send Kelsey to a private school, Leslie said that she didn't have reliable transportation to get her to and from school safely, and that the anti-lock brakes on her car were faulty and locked up every time that she hit the brake. Knowing that at any moment, that could cause an accident, I made a deal with my ex-wife that if my daughter was to attend there, I would give her $5000 toward the purchase of a vehicle of her choosing, however, my daughter was to attend the school. I helped my ex-wife and my daughter drive around to find a vehicle. We looked on the internet, and several other dealerships in the area, and surrounding area, and I drove them over to there to find the vehicle. About half way through our searching, we stopped by mammaw's house to relax for a bit. At this time mammaw had been passed away about 2 weeks. The house felt empty without her being there. I went over and sat on the far side of the couch, Mary and James in one of the chairs in the living room. Leslie took the other chair, and Gerald sat on the opposite couch from me. Kelsey was the next to sit down. As soon as she sat down, she laid her head right over on Gerald. Do you have any idea how insulting and degrading that was to me? Here I was, helping them get a vehicle, getting Kelsey in a new school for her betterment of education, and I even had bought Kelsey a bouquet of flowers while we were out, and that is the respect and gratitude that she had to show me. I was doing everything that I could do to help them, just like I had over the years, yet they never had the courtesy to show any gratitude. I stood up off the couch, and walked right out the back door to the back porch. It was better than raising my voice, as that really made me upset. I sat out on the back porch and turned on the TV, just to get away from Kelsey. Oh man, I was livid with them. The next thing, about 2 minutes later, Kelsey comes out of the door onto the back porch and wants to sit on my lap. The "only" reason why she did that, is because Mary called her out in front of her mom and Gerald of how rude that was. I was so mad at her when she came out there, that I told her to just go back in the house and leave me alone. When someone upsets me like that, the best thing they can do is leave me alone and let me cool off.

They finally located a vehicle that was going to be good in the winter snow, and as well throughout the summer months, and they settled on the vehicle. I called my bank to verify my funds, went to my banks branch office in Ohio and had a Cashier's Check drawn up to the dealership for the vehicle. The next thing my ex-wife knows, she is driving around in a newer model Ford, and I was relieved that I knew my daughter was going to be safe getting back and forth to school. Needless to say, just like every other attempt I made at making my daughter's life, just a little bit easier, went right out the window. My daughter never stepped foot in that school, and immediately following, another incident took place. These people were lucky that I didn't back out of the deal myself and have them get their own vehicle after the way that Kelsey had been treating me. Have you ever seen that sign "Bang Head Here?" Yes, after all of the trouble and money, it was all for nothing. Well wait a minute, my ex-wife got a free car out of the deal, which was a complete farce, because she lied to me in order to get it. How many of you would be completely irked after handing over $5000 for a car to be used for transportation to a private school, and then the kid gets nothing out of it, not even the education that she deserves?

Shortly thereafter, given my hectic and utterly insane work schedule, I drove over to Eastern Kentucky for a visit to see my daughter and take her to one of the most amazing planetariums that you would ever care to visit. It is a big dome building, with floor projectors and a dome ceiling. You lay back in the chairs and it takes you on one of the coolest space exploration journeys. Frankly, they should have something like this at Disney or Universal Studios in my opinion, because as much as I liked it, I am sure there are others that would love to see it. After driving a long 3 hours to get over to Eastern Kentucky, and 20 minutes from my daughter's house, I called her up letting her know that I was coming to get her, and she said, "I don't want to come with you, I want to go over to pappaws", which is her step-dad's dad and she wanted to play in the creek. Now, did you get that? She would rather me drive all the way over to see her, and tell me to go home, because she just wanted to go over to her "pappaws" and play in the creek. She even knew why I was there, because I told her. She didn't care not one single bit, when I just spent the evening driving to see her. Who here would be madder than a wet hen over that one?

Chapter 30 - The Greedy and the Proud!

Have you ever been unlucky enough to meet somebody who was so greedy, sitting around the dinner table, that you couldn't even get a bite to eat yourself? You're the one who cooked it, you're the one who served it, and you can't even get a bite to eat of the meal that you put out there, because there was nothing left to get. Remember earlier that I was mentioning people who didn't want to work but wanted the best of everything? How many of you would agree that we should just hand over our hard earned money?

Just a few years prior, there was a "child support review" that was started by my ex-wife and the child support office, because I was working and making a little bit more money. I contacted my ex-wife and told her that I didn't have the time to take vacation and come deal with this nonsense in court. I drove out to the child support office and met with her and the lady in the office, and told them that I would gladly give my ex-wife an extra $1000 a year, to cover child expenses such as clothes, field trips, etc., since she was calling me all of the time anyway asking for this money. For several years, after filing taxes, I would call Leslie up, and inform her that I was sending that money, and then it got to the point where I purchased a joint Wal-Mart card, sent her one, and would load the money onto the account with the other so I didn't have to send it by mail using a money order. It was much easier to manage for me. In April or May, can't remember the exact date, in 2011, when I got my tax money refund, I called my ex-wife and informed her that I had the money to load on the card, and she told me that she didn't want the money yet. I told her, as any prudent person would, that I couldn't just hold onto the money, because I had a lot of activities and moving parts going on, in and around, at my office.

I explained to her that if she didn't take the money now, then I couldn't guarantee to her that I would have the money later. She insisted that I "hold" onto the money "for her". I told her straight out, "Listen Leslie, I am not the International Bank of Cleland", and I did not function as a bank account where, "she could just walk in anytime you wanted and make a withdrawal." The point to this was, it was her money, and I was delivering it to her, as agreed upon, but she wasn't willing to take the money. In June or July, she contacted me expecting me to have the money "readily" available for her, and I didn't have the money, as I figured I wouldn't in earlier months, because of the constant flux of money at my office. She went off on me and was furious, because I couldn't simply just hand it over to her. What can I say? I did warn her at the time, that I may or may not have the money later on down the road when she asked. There were points when I would do my company expenses that I would send to the credit card company, anywhere between $5000-$7000 dollars in a 2 week period, from the filing of my travel expense reports, so when I say there was a lot of moving parts, there really were.

Have you ever heard of David Copperfield? He is one of the greatest magicians in the world. He has made airplanes disappear, right in front of your very eyes. A lot of this is smoke and mirrors, but at the same time, it takes a lot of talent to create the illusion. In dealing with my ex-wife, there has been a lot of smoke and mirrors over the years. In August of 2012, my ex-wife decides to take me back to court for child support. As if I wasn't helping enough, she decided that she was going to get greedy, and put more undue stress on my family, simply because, later in 2011, I couldn't just manifest the extra money she wanted me to "hold" for her. My father had warned her in the past about such an incident and explained to her that if I lost my job as a result of anything, then she wouldn't be getting any money whatsoever for child support, along with all of the other help my family and I have rendered to her, due to Kelsey, over the years. I spoke with my ex-wife about this and told her that if she would stop this moronic child support review, I would send her about $4500 from my brokerage account. I didn't want to really do this, but it was cheaper than me having to take off work to go deal with, yet another problem. I signed into my brokerage account, issued the check to be sent to her, and what do you know, Leslie didn't follow through with her end of the deal. I sat down, drank me a cup of coffee and thought clearly about what was going on. A couple of days later I went back in and issued a stop payment on the check. Why? Because firstly, I don't like to be led along, secondly I hate being lied to, and lastly because the issuance of such a check could be considered bribery in court, although that is clearly not what I had intended it to be. Since I wasn't going to get the courtesy from Leslie, I wasn't going to continue to extend my courtesy any further.

About 2 weeks later, just keeping up with my ex-wife's predictable behavior, I get a nasty gram from the county attorney threatening me, because I put a stop payment on the check, for theft by deception. I talked to my attorney's office and they laughed at that, because that is not even close to what it was. I was well within my legal rights to put a stop payment on the check, because I didn't purchase goods or services. I checked with several other local banks on the responsibilities of accounts, and they informed me that it is the account holder's responsibility, not another party, to ensure that the checks issued clear prior to usage. My attorneys sent a letter back to the county attorney, in no less terms than telling him to kiss my butt, because he didn't have a leg to stand on. What happened? Leslie received the check, deposited it at her local bank, and they immediately credited her account for all of the money. The standard operating procedures at banking institutions, is a hold of money, until the check can be verified, which could take upwards of 7-14 days. She immediately went out, once they credited her account, prematurely, and spent every last dime of what the check was made out for. Flittering money is never a good idea. The repercussion of what she did overdrew her bank account for the total of the check and overdraft fees. I am sorry, but she shouldn't have tried to take advantage of my family, at the expense of Mary or James or even my baby girl Katie, knowing that most likely none of the money was being used on Kelsey.

Up till this point in my life, in the pursuit of my career, things were looking great. I was able to afford to help my daughter when she needed the extra boost, and I had a few different personal credit cards to float some money in the event of emergencies. I had my company credit card for Nuance that I was using for expenses for travel and office needs, and things were just perfect. At any point in time, I could afford a few hundred dollars to throw here or there. Leslie would still, up to this point, call me up periodically telling me that she didn't have money for certain things, such as field trips, pictures, or other items, and I would help her out. There was one time that she called me up, and asked me if I had $300 that she could get from me, so she could buy Kelsey a trampoline. I said ok, and sent her the money but also told her to not mention that the money came from me, but rather her. I didn't want my daughter thinking that her mother could not afford it, and I wanted her to think it come from her mother. She, to this day, still does not know that these items actually come from me. In the winter months, around November of 2012, just 3 months after the increase in child support, there was a time that I was visiting my ex-wife and Kelsey and Leslie was out of money, and destitute, and wasn't able to afford buying any groceries at her home. Keep in mind, she was on government food-stamps and still ran out of money. Apparently there was a bit of waste at her house, otherwise there would have been plenty of food to be had. I took Leslie, in snow, all of the way around to town and got out $300, in cash, took her to the grocery store, and a few other stops, and then back to her house. I know, I shouldn't have been that kind, but after all, Kelsey was living with her at the time; and I didn't want my daughter going hungry. What other ex-husband, who has been through what I have been, would have been nice enough to do that? Not many that I can think of.

Immediately following the assistance I rendered to my ex-wife, came yet another traumatizing event in my life, on November 10th 2012. My mammaw Lila was like a second mother to me. She took care of me from the time I was months old, and we were always very close. As you have read, I spent a lot of time with my mammaw and thought the world of her. I believe I was coming from my ex-wife's or thereabouts when I got the phone call that mammaw had contracted a string of pneumonia and had been admitted to ICU in Ashland, Kentucky at the hospital. By the time I made it there, the whole family was there, from aunts to uncles and cousins, my second cousins were even there. My father, who was of ill health in Florida, was not able to come; however, he made me keep in close contact with him on the phone; so he knew what was going on. At the time, my mammaw was 92 years old and had raised all of her children and most of the grandchildren including me. She wasn't that educated, more than my grandfather; but she was well educated in taking care of the kids. I remember as clear as it was yesterday, because she was in an isolated room, oxygen mask on, and tubes everywhere. She had to have oxygen, because her lungs were filled with fluid. I walked over, grabbed my mammaw's hand and stood there looking at her, as she was me. I remember that I told her how much I loved her, and that I would not leave. I remember that she told me to make sure I was back on Saturday.

The family took turns rotating between mammaw's home, and the hospital, to make sure that she was being watched over properly, and to call and inform the rest of the family if there was any change. On Sunday November 11th 2012, mammaw slipped into a deep sleep, because of how weak she was, at her age, fighting the infection in her lungs. The family knew that she was not going to be around much longer, so it was at that time she was moved to the local hospice center, where we could spend the last remaining hours with her. Again, the whole family came to the hospice center; and we stayed for a long time throughout the day. At this point, the nurses at the facility had her on manual oxygen without an automatic breather so she could try to breathe on her own. My uncle and I stayed overnight at the hospice center in case anything was to happen. This went on until Monday evening, when everyone was exhausted, and stayed over at my mammaw's house, and again, my uncle and I stayed with my grandmother, sitting beside her bed. At the time, my uncle was asleep in his chair, and I stayed awake, holding my mammaw's fragile hand. At around 1:10 AM on November 13th, she started wheezing, and barely breathing, and I woke my uncle up and went down the hall in a hurry to get the nurse at the desk. She took the oxygen mask off, and at 2:34 AM, my mammaw drew her last breath on earth.

I don't know how to describe being beside your close family member, watching an era pass right in front of your very eyes, but you could sense her soul coming out of her body. My uncle and I paused for a short time, as the nurse left the room, so we could have a moment with a precious loved one. My father asked me to take some pictures of his mother, so he could grieve as well. I reluctantly took the pictures, but did because I was under orders of my father to do so, and emailed them to dad. I called up the family, and informed them of the passing; and my uncle and I went home for some rest. The following Friday, November 16th, was my mammaw's funeral. There were 92 people at the funeral, family and friends. The cousins and I, all of which were her 1st grandsons, were the pallbearers, escorted my mammaw's casket to the burial grounds, and sat her down. It was a very emotional time for me, because of who she was, what she did for the family and I, as well as the fact she also took care of Kelsey. Kelsey was her great granddaughter.

While I was at her home in November, I had Mary with me, along with James and Katie, my other little angel. We were all at Leslie's home, and I suggested that we all go out. While we were out, I took everyone for dinner at McDonald's in Ohio, just down the road from the roller-skating rink. There was Leslie, Kelsey, Priscilla and her daughter, Mary, James, Katie and I, which was a nice sized cost for dinner. We sat around the tables and had fun while we were there eating. At the time, Kelsey was 14 years old; and she was laughing and carrying on, just like any other happy teenager. Leslie, Priscilla, Mary and I, sat around the table talking while we were there, and nothing seemed out of order at all. Once we were done there, we all left and went to the roller-skating rink, where again, I paid for all of our admissions, skates and snacks. We skated for a few hours, while the time was getting late outside. I used to be quite a skater when I was younger; however, as I got older, apparently my balance abilities went right out the window. I tried my best to get out there and skate and I did, but I wiped out several times and hit the floor, and the wall.

I tripped several times, landed on my face, my knees and tore a hole in one of my brand new pair of jeans, right at my knee, and ended up with a friction burn. The whole reason why we went out, was so that I could spend some time with my daughter Kelsey, and so we could just hang out, talk, and have some fun along the way. Kelsey would skate up to me, and we would talk for a minute, and I would go out to skate with her. As soon as I got out there, Kelsey would take off and leave me skating by myself. I would wait on her, or catch up and she would do the same thing to me, giving me the cold shoulder. After about an hour or so of that, I will admit, I got pretty upset at her, because that was supposed to be some time we were going to spend together, and what do I get except the smirk, rolled eyes, and an ungrateful attitude. Eventually, I skated over to the counter, handed in my skates, so I could get my shoes back, and went back over to the lockers to get my jacket out. I went outside to get some air and cool off a little bit, since it was hot in the rink. They stayed there another 45 minutes or so, then everyone was ready to go. They all may have had fun, but after being blown off by my own daughter, I didn't feel that she really wanted to be there much at all, especially with me or parents in general.

Also, around this same time frame, while visiting my ex-wife's home, Mary noticed some things as well, and also I learned some interesting facts that came right out of the mouths of my ex-wife's husband as well. I can't remember exactly where I was, maybe outside, and I learned about this as a result of Mary telling me later. Kelsey was talking to her mother like a dog, smartmouthing her, not minding, not even being respectful in the least. Here sat Mary, and Gerald spoke up and said, "You're not going to let her talk to you like that are you?" Apparently so, because my ex-wife didn't retaliate at all from what Mary said. Wow, are you serious? My ex-wife wouldn't correct my child, how interesting isn't it? Shortly after that, while actually trying to help Gerald with some programming, he told me some more interesting information. One morning, Kelsey was giving him a hard time about going to school and had locked herself in the bathroom, and wouldn't get on the bus, as it was almost to where she got on at. He ended up breaking down the bathroom door, and Kelsey fell back on the floor.

It was a little more than I would have done personally, but kids need to mind adults. When she got to school, she complained to the teachers and principal that he had hit her in the face with his hand. From what I gather, several State Police, and CPS people showed up to the school, and would not let her go home at the end of the day, and in addition, questioned Gerald and Leslie. Now, it's pretty obvious if you look at the size of him that if he had actually hit her, she would have a swollen face, possible broken bones and a black eye, but that just simply wasn't the case. Kelsey lied her butt off to the authorities, just to get attention, or something. Who knows what the real reason was at the time, because I was lucky to even find that information out. He even bragged to me one day about punching Leslie in the face, because she was running her mouth to him, and she buckled up and hit the floor like a dead weight. As long as she and I had been together, and all of the problems that we had, I wouldn't ever have hit her, although on a couple of cases I sure felt like it. One more interesting fact I picked up, was that while myself and Leslie were remotely dating while I was first stationed at Quantico that she was sleeping with another guy back where she lived, and I never found out about it, till just then, 15 years later. That kind of information makes a man think doesn't it, if you catch my drift? That made a total of 3 guys that she slept with, that I found out about, the time that we were together. If there were others, I never heard about it, but honestly, I was glad to be rid of that woman, if you want to call her that. The real term to describe the total of behavior is a Succubus.

Chapter 31 - You Expect Me to Pay How Much?

Ok, I mentioned that Leslie took me back to court in August of 2012 for more child support, but I never told you much more than that. Let me take some time here and expound on a few things which I left out. Up until this point, I was not only paying a "reasonable" amount of child support; but I was also giving my ex-wife an extra $1000 a year, and furthermore helping her with "extras" that she would come to me with, throughout the year. I didn't mind to help out with some one-off's when needed, for my daughter Kelsey, because I loved the little thing more than life itself, as with all of my children. It is a father's prerogative to help their child, and that is what I exercised. Although, Kelsey was ungrateful of a lot that has been done for her, I thought that one of these days, she would grow out of it, and realize that daddy was doing the best he could for her.

After the court date, I went from paying a reasonable amount, to nearly $900 a month for one single child who could care less about seeing her father, spending time with him, or for that matter, picking up the phone and calling me. I told Leslie, as well as my father and Mary that the expectation of me paying that much in child support was impossible and I couldn't afford that every single month. Granted, I was making much better money than in previous years, but I couldn't afford that much money for myself every month, let alone paying that money out in child support, which I knew wasn't going for my daughter.

Now, prior to November of 2012, no one, including Leslie, told me that she had gone out and bought herself a new double wide trailer. No one gave me the courtesy of letting me know that they had moved from their rented home in Eastern Kentucky, and no one bothered to let me know that they were even planning on moving. Why was I taken back to court to pay excessive child support? Because my ex-wife was living beyond her means, and decided to make a move on buying a home, and didn't care what "damage" she was going to cause my family by doing so. My ex-wife told me later that when she moved into her new house that she made a deal with her 18 year old sister that she would pay half the monthly payments on the house. What grown adult of 29 years old, in their logical mind, would think that an 18 year old, of any kind, would carry through with something of that magnitude? I would have understood something like paying you back a $500 loan, or something like a cheap car, but splitting a house payment every single month. That whole situation was really not good judgment.

The entertainment of such an idea is humorous at the least and ridiculous at the most, but still, Leslie decided that was what she was going to trust her sister with. That agreement didn't last but a month or two, and then her sister left her holding the proverbial bill with her house, like that is a surprise. The "persona" she puts onto everyone is that she is this perfect, down to earth, churchgoing person who will help others, namely herself; but she wouldn't admit to that, nor would she ever let on what her real plans were. For this matter, supposedly she was taking Kelsey to "church" as well, but their actions differ. This person type is known as prevaricate, and is defined as "to speak falsely or misleadingly; deliberately misstate or create an incorrect impression; lie." according to defined terms; the holding of information, with the intention to deceive. How can you cure this? Well, from what I have dealt with over the years, I don't know of any cure, or even relief of symptoms from this behavior, as it has only gotten worse, and I don't mean just in money terms either.

Chapter 32 - Christmas, the Most Unhappy Time of the Year!

I have had a lot of good and happy Christmases over the years, with my immediate family growing up, and spending time with other friends and relatives, whom were important, integral parts of my life. I wanted my family to share the same feelings with each other, to share the same memories, to share the same holiday cheer, and to be interactive with one another. I wanted my daughter Kelsey to spend time with my family, Mary, James, and her sister Katie, as well as get to know, a little better, Mary's parents, whom are technically her Step Grandparents, since Mary and I had been together, at this point, over 9 years. Mary and her family have done their best to make their home available and open to Kelsey when she come down to visit and talk with her, like part of the family.

In December of 2012, I called my attorney's office, and spoke with them about my rights, to Kelsey, as I wanted to make sure I was legally covered to be able to see my daughter. After speaking with my attorney, he advised me to go ahead and drive over and get my daughter, which I gladly did, because I really wanted to spend some time with her over Christmas; and I wanted her to spend time with her siblings. Why would I do that? Well it boils down to the problems Leslie was giving me, in seeing my daughter, and putting it in my daughter's mind that she was better off not seeing me. Apparently, in her mind, that is her daughter, and only her daughter and I didn't have any say so, in her upbringing, or in her clothes she wore, or her internet presence, or anything else for that matter. If you have been following along, doesn't that seem apparent to you? I was utterly disappointed in the fact, I would even have to call my attorney to ask, rather than just communicating with my ex-wife over the matter, and having her cooperate with me, since I was entitled to see my daughter and wasn't able to see my daughter for several holidays, due to my schedule or her not allowing me to come and see her.

It was an embarrassment to me, since Mary had been with me for 9 of 14 years of Kelsey's live, and it was hard on me to be away from Kelsey, alone having her mother putting all of this nonsense in her head about daddy. So I did exactly what my attorney's office suggested I do, and I called my ex-wife and politely demanded to her that she have my daughter ready, because I was going to come pick her up for Christmas. She said, "Kelsey doesn't want to see you for Christmas", so again I politely and firmly recommended she have Kelsey ready. The way I looked at this whole thing, was, "Hey, if I am going to have to pay $900 a month in child support, then I had better get to see my daughter", because she was my child, and I loved the little thing. She was my flesh and blood, and a child whom I hoped to have good ethics instilled in, at least a little.

I have to be honest up front. This was the worst Christmas that I have ever had, let alone most other people's holidays. What I was about ready to deal with has really turned my family upside down, because of the arrogance, lies and deceptions that have been put out there. I certainly don't appreciate it, and it has caused a lot of grief in my family, hard feelings. That Christmas Mary, Katie, James and I, packed up our vehicle and drove to Eastern Kentucky to pick up my daughter for Christmas. The plan was to drop off Mary and the kids in Tennessee, and then myself and my daughter drive to Central Kentucky to spend Christmas together. Since I had not seen Kelsey for several holidays, I wanted it to be just me and her. For me, it was important to be able to spend time with my daughter. For any father who loves his children that is something that he wants to do. Kelsey and I were going to spend Christmas together, and then travel down to Tennessee to where Mary and the kids were, and have Christmas there as well.

After we drove three and a half hours to pick up my daughter, all of us drove down to Tennessee as planned, dropped them off, and we continued towards Central Kentucky just as planned. On the way, just like always, Kelsey was playing with my cellphone. I kept a lock code on my smartphone, because I didn't want James and Katie getting in it, and erasing something. Kelsey on the other hand was sneaky, as always, and every chance she got, she was trying to see what my lock code was, when I wasn't paying attention. Apparently, that was what happened, because when I looked over, she was in my phone nosing around. Honestly I had forgotten what all was in my smartphone at the time, but there was some pictures that I definitely didn't want her seeing. The next thing I know, she found the pictures of my deceased mammaw, her great grandmother. I grabbed the phone and said I didn't want you to see that, because I didn't want to expose her to something of that emotional level. Her response to me was, "I've seen worse." This was the same grandmother who took care of her since she was 3, and the same grandmother who watched over her when I had to go out. This was the same grandmother who loved her to death, because she was my child; she didn't have not a sign of remorse, not a sniffle, not a tear or nothing. Her face was as cold as ice. That really hurt me, because she was supposed to love this woman. I was floored, stumped, and completely caught off guard by her response, and I honestly didn't know what to say to her about it. This was the most heinous 3 days that I have ever spent with my daughter. I have never in my life received the cold shoulder the way that she had been treating me during this time, from anybody else. She refused to talk to me, and would get irritated when I would ask to speak with her about anything. For the first 24 hours after we got to Central Kentucky at my home, I turned on some TV, made her dinner, and sat down on the floor with her to try and enjoy the evening. She wouldn't eat anything, apparently, because she didn't like my cooking. I don't know if it was that, or she was just irritated because she actually had to come spend time with her father. What's really bothersome to me is that she really used to enjoy spending time with me. She used to be "daddy this and daddy that", because all she ever wanted was her dad.

There were years that went by, that she consistently asked me why her mother and I cannot be together, or asked why we were not married anymore. If she only knew the real reason why we could not be married anymore, she would understand the answer to that question. If she only realized how bad her mother had treated me over the years, and what she has done to my daughter, she would also understand the reason to that question. Being a good father, most of the things that I have been put through over the years, I have hidden from her because I didn't want her to think bad of her mother, and even if I did tell her she most likely would not believe me, as she has been living with her mother all these years. It is one of those situations where you could not possibly believe as a child that your parent, especially your mother, could be a bad person, and that is my opinion. I know that I have made mistakes along the way raising my daughter, when I was allowed to; but I still love my daughter no matter what she has done to my family.

The next day, she and I went out on a drive to Louisville Kentucky, close by the mall. We didn't have anything else to do, so I took her shopping in the mall. To show you what type of isolation this poor girl had during her life living with her mother, once we walked into the mall she said and I quote, "where are the shopping carts?" I couldn't help but to laugh, but I told her that this is a mall, not a department store.   I tried to explain to her up front that when you go shopping in a mall, there are many different stores, not just one. I also explained to her that when you go shopping in a mall usually they give you bags that you carry out to your car, from the respective stores that you go in. She didn't catch what I was meaning right off, but after a couple of visits into different stores, she started to understand. It is no wonder coming from where she was living that she didn't grasp the concept of what a mall was. We went from store to store just browsing; because I wanted to show my daughter and that there was more to life than just simple department stores. After several stores, she found one that she liked. It was a shoe store, which she decided that she liked – go figure. She went in and looked at all variety of shoes, and picked her out a pair that she really wanted. We made it up to the checkout attendant, and hearing these ostrich skin boots up. I'm not even sure what they're called, I think "Uggs", apparently they're pretty popular with the kids, but they cost about $300 a pair.

I didn't know what to think when he rang those up, but I decided that that is what she wanted and that was what she was going to get, so I got out my credit card and made the purchase. From there we went to a jewelry store, and she bought a necklace that she liked.   We left there and browsed around on the second floor of the mall where they had different types of trinkets, statues, pretty much anything that you want. She found a horse clock that was fairly expensive as well, but she likes horses, so I got it for her room. She also headed to the girls clothes section, where she tried on a lot of different outfits. Once we were done with that store she had done spent about $400 more. After all of the shopping was done we went back to my house to let me try to relax from all of the spending. That evening cost me around $800 just in shopping, not to mention what I had already spent for Christmas. Once we got back to my house, I flopped on the couch, and Kelsey decided that she was going to try on all of her clothes.

I was really proud of her for picking out some conservative clothes, because of her previous terrible choice of clothes. She really looked good in her new clothes, and it was a hot look that she would fit right in with the preppy crowd. When I was younger, I dressed so hot that a person's eyes would catch on fire if they looked at me too long. Yea, I know, that is funny, but it's the truth. During the course of this, I happened to be in my office at the house, doing some studying on the computer, and Kelsey came in there with her new Apple IPOD Touch. She was acting really funny because earlier when we first got there, she asked if she could put it on the internet there, so she could listen to music. I let her, since that was a good reason, and I didn't know much about the IPOD but I learn pretty quickly, considering it is a lot like an IPhone. I asked her if I could see it, and boy she was really acting strange about it. She was standing over my shoulder, breathing down my neck and had a strange look on her face. I pretended like I didn't know much about it at that point, because I wanted to find out exactly why she was acting so funny. Only time would tell. She had that IPOD locked down with a 30 character passphrase, and there was no way on earth I could crack through it, because I sure as heck tried after she went to sleep. Privacy doesn't exist when you are managing a sneaky kid who apparently has something to hide from you. I didn't care then, and I don't care now, because I would do the same thing to my son, or my youngest daughter Katie. My kids had better come forward and stand tall with me, or I will find out on my own. If I have to do the later, I will be furious.

That evening after I had relaxed, she told me that she was bored and wanted something to do. I was hoping that she was not going to tell me that she wanted to go shopping again. We went by one of the restaurants locally, and got some ice cream cones, and ate them on the way to Louisville. She wanted to go out to do something, so I suggested that we go ice skating. We went ice skating, both of our first times, it didn't take her long to catch the hang of it, however, it did take me a while. I ended up falling on my face a number of times, falling on my back and ended up hurting my back, my knee and my elbow. I didn't want to show any pain, so I got back up and kept going. We were there a good couple of hours, and she seemed to really enjoy herself. Once we were done there we left to go home and get some rest for the night. I know one thing; I slept well that night, because I was so darn tired from skating. If you know what I mean, the older you get, the less it takes to tire you, so I went home, Kelsey hit the couch and I hit the bed. I didn't even remember falling asleep like normally, I was just out cold. The next day, Kelsey hit the bathroom, and tried on all of her outfits. I was proud, for once, that she picked out conservative clothes, not revealing clothes, that didn't leave anything to the imagination. She had a tendency in the past, to wear stuff that I sure didn't approve of, and mostly at her mother's discretion, which wasn't much in my opinion.

The next day, we went ice skating again, went to get more ice cream, and hit the trail behind one of the local schools, just to go for a walk and talk. I did my best to give her good sound advice about the boys. I explained to her that boys her age are usually out for one thing nowadays, and that she needed to be careful. I explained to her that they would tell her anything, including that they loved her, just to get it, and then kick her butt off to the curb. I didn't hide anything, I didn't sugar coat anything either. I figure if my kid is going to go out into the warzone, she better be prepared for what is coming. Marines don't go out to the warfront without knowing what they are going to be looking at when they get there, who is going to be coming at them, or what weapons they are going to encounter. If anything, they have all of this information up front, and they also have a terrain map, aerial photos, and half the time, they already know where the enemy is dug in before they hit the ground hot ready to kill anything that moves. The point that I am making, as a father who cares, is that I wasn't about ready, for 1 single second, going to send my kid unknowingly into that world, without advising her about what she was walking into. I didn't trust my ex-wife to do it then, still don't trust her now, and will never trust her to do the right thing, or watch out for my kid's back. I didn't want my daughter getting pregnant at a young age, and then remembering what dad said about things. I didn't want her ruining her life at a young age, by having a kid too soon, not having its father around, or for that matter, not caring about his child, and leaving her with all of the responsibilities.

So here we were, at my place, or at least out running around having a good time, and I was miserable. She had me in tears most of the time she was there, because of how she was treating me, like a third rate piece of trash. To her, I was nothing but a guy, not her father, not anything important, not even a passerby on the street. How could a father, who loves his child so much, and spent all of the time she was alive, have a daughter like that, who could care less about him? Who knows, but it's not on account of me not trying. Care to take a guess of what the underlying problem was? Do I even need to come out and say it? Listen folks, my daughter is important to me, just like I said before, and like I will say now. I couldn't take the tears and feeling isolated with her alone anymore, so instead of staying at my house for Christmas, we packed up the car, and went back down to Tennessee where I didn't have to be alone with her by myself, and where at least I had my other 2 babies that wanted to talk to dad. We got down there and spent the night.

The next morning we got up, and it was Christmas day. We all got up and the kids opened their presents. Now while we were at

Mary's parents that day, Kelsey was all chipper, smiles on her face, and was having a great time. Little Katie was only about 7 months old at the time, and this was the first time Kelsey had been able to see and spend time with her little sister. To me, it was very important that these 2 sisters get acquainted because later in life, they were going to need each other. For anyone who has sisters, you know what I mean. Kelsey went into the bedroom where Mary was, and played with Katie, and held her and gave her the pacifier. Katie was always particular about having a pacifier with her, because it kept her calm. Once she was done there, we went out to the living room and opened presents. Half the time, Kelsey was sitting on my lap in the chair, leg falling asleep, because she was so heavy, but I was enjoying it, because Kelsey was in a good mood, and wasn't making me feel like a piece of trash she was going to just throw away. That evening Kelsey and I went out to the mall parking lot late at night, so there wouldn't be anyone around to run into and I let her drive my car to get some practice in. While we were out there, we were talking about a variety of topics, but one specifically stood out in my mind, and that was porn. Apparently Kelsey had found one of her younger brother's porn magazines at her mother's home and was sitting there flipping through it. I asked her who it belonged to and she said her younger brother. Upon inquiring further about it, Gerald had given it to his boy, who wasn't but about 9 or 10 at the time. Kelsey didn't seem to think much of it, nor was she embarrassed that she just literally came out and told me about it. Does anything seem wrong with that picture to you?

We had our Christmas at Mary's parents and spent the day with the kids, and then the kids crashed out for the night. On the way to Tennessee I had remembered Kelsey had told me that she removed the passcode on her IPOD, and I figured I would take advantage of the situation. I snuck into the bedroom where Kelsey was guarding her IPOD like the stash of gold at Ft. Knox and took it to the computer and commenced working on it. I hooked it up to WiFi, and immediately I started receiving messages from some kid calling my daughter bunny, and telling her how sexy she was asking for more pictures of her. I told the kid that the IPOD had crashed and asked him to send my pictures back to me that I had already sent him. WOW! Here my daughter was taking provocative pictures of herself and sending them to this kid. I was downright mad. I called up Leslie and talked to her about this, and she didn't know that you could message on an IPOD, which is what we had tried to prevent, but instead of Leslie asking me in advance, she shot gunned it, and got her something to get in more trouble with.

The next morning we took Kelsey home to her mothers, and then went back to our home in central Kentucky. We spent a lot of time on the road, but being able to see my kid, was well worth the drive, but I sure wish she wouldn't have made me feel so bad about being around her earlier. Any idea how it feels to be around someone who doesn't want to be around you? Yea, that is the feeling I had for 3 whole days, and it frankly sucked. Mary, James, Katie, and I traveled back to central Kentucky at that point to have Christmas as a family again at our home, and James and Katie had fun, yet again, ripping into the presents that Santa left under the tree while they were gone to mammaw's. There is nothing that gives me more satisfaction and happiness than seeing my children enjoying themselves. Mary and I sat in the floor taking pictures of these two little ones, and helping Katie get the hang of shredding her presents open. The little thing was just a baby, so it was going to take some help for her to really get into the swing of things, although after showing her how to, she took right off opening them up.

The following 2 weekends, Mary, James, Katie, and I went to my ex-wife's home, setting aside my better judgment, so that I could spend more time with Kelsey, because I wanted to. I wanted Kelsey to not feel like her brother and sister were more important than she was and didn't want them to feel less important, and didn't want James or Katie feeling like they couldn't have any opportunities to get to know their older sister. Although Kelsey was my first, she certainly wasn't my last, yet she was the oldest and I figured she understood how important her siblings were to her. These 2 weekends I cooked at my ex-wife's, went to the store and got snacks, sat around with my ex-wife, her friend Priscilla, and Mary and talked. Mary said that most of the time she was there, my ex-wife was pumping her for personal information about me, us and the kids, which I didn't know about till a little while later after we left. While we were there, we watched movies, played card games, and laughed around a lot.

What I was really hoping, although, I knew something later would come up of some reason or another, was that "for the sake of the kids", I could get along with my ex-wife and find a reason to spend some quality time with my daughter. One of the days, and again, I didn't know about this till later either, I walked out back of my ex-wife's home to get some air, was kicking some twigs around, looking at the mountains, and Kelsey said, "Why is he out there being stupid". Ok, first off, that was rude and second of all Mary told me this after we had left. Why on earth would being outside make me stupid? What really irked me was Kelsey calling me Cleland. Oh heck no, you are not going to do that, although she had been pulling this for the last year. She got to the point where she went from being my sweet loving baby girl, to a downright disrespectful twerp who was really making me ill. I spoke to my ex-wife about it, and although she said that she didn't agree with it, I could tell that she was enjoying the fact that my daughter was turning on me. Kelsey also had also been calling me ugly, and fat, which I am not, at least not what most people tell me. One day, she told me I was ugly, and I said, "you look just like me, so that makes you ugly too", and she responded with an offended tone. I am not sure what she expected? I also had a thorough talk with Leslie about what I found on her IPOD and with Leslie's permission, tore Kelsey's room apart looking for any type of leads as to what was going on. In the process, I found a pair of Victoria's Secret thong laced tan panties that her aunt Cassandra had given her. Now, why does a 14 year old need underwear like that? For that matter, why did Cassandra give them to her at all? Listen folks, call me old fashioned, but I don't think it is appropriate for a 14 year old girl to be wearing something like that. From what I recall, Leslie didn't take them away from her, or throw them away, but that particular memory isn't fully vivid.

While I was there at my ex-wife's with my family, Kelsey and her friend wanted to go out hiking the hills next to their house. I was exhausted already, but I wanted her to have fun, so I went along to make sure they would be alright. When we were on the way back, I was walking along side of my daughter and she hit me right across the back of my calves with a large stick she had found, for no apparent reason. I am telling you, it hurt and I had a big bruise across my legs because of it. I have no idea why she would do something like that, but I just kept my mouth shut and didn't get mad about it. Honestly, it was too cold outside for me to get upset at that moment in time.

Chapter 33 - The Ex-Wife Who Would Stop at Nothing

You know, there are those people whom you can't make happy no matter how hard you tried, and then there is Mary. Mary has had it wonderful since we have been together. Most of the time, I do the cleaning around the house, about 50% of the time I do the cooking too. I love cleaning the house and doing the laundry, which I have never had a problem doing. Since Mary and I have been together, we would go on vacation 2 or 3 times a year, and visit some of the most amazing places together. Why? Because I earned it and worked hard to get to that point in my life that I could enjoy it with my children. Did Kelsey go? No, because her mother found every excuse in the book to not let her go. One of the big ones was, well since my son can't do these things, then I don't think it's fair that Kelsey do that either. Here is some news for you! You should be thankful and glad her dad takes an interest in her enough to want to take her out and do these things; otherwise she might be like a million other children whose fathers don't care.

In the first weeks of January 2013, just following our terrible Christmas, and visit to my "ex-wife's humble abode", and right smack dab in the middle of my work day, I get the call to end all calls from my wonderful ex-wife. I swear, up until this point, I didn't think anything could get much worse; but boy I was wrong. My ex-wife preached the gospel according to Leslie all of these years that I needed to spend time with Kelsey. She acted like I never come to see her, and that I never spent any time with Kelsey. I would say that in my position, working as a father should, and the distance I had to travel to see my daughter, I did a pretty good job at spending time with Kelsey, and providing for her. So here I am sitting behind my desk, Mary in there talking with me already, and I get this phone call. Leslie, went around to the Child Protective Services office, and told them that I said my daughter was hot and sexy and that I wanted in her pants. How can I even say this; wow. I told Leslie straight up on the phone, "Are you completely out of your bloody mind", and "You have single handedly destroyed my relationship with my daughter." I couldn't believe what I was hearing from this person. As if it wasn't hard enough trying to be there for my daughter, my ex-wife in her infinite wisdom decides to pull a grenade out and throw it at me. Sure I told my daughter what warzone she was going to be walking into with the opposite sex, but

I will be darned if I told her that "I" thought of her that way. She was my kid and an important one at that. If it wasn't bad enough that Leslie did that, she called me up to "rub" it in my face. I had my ex-wife clearly state to me one day that she was living life through my daughter, simply because she didn't get to experience a lot of things when she was younger, which is a very bad move on the part of a parent. What was really strange about the whole incident was that myself and my ex-wife were working on getting my daughter into Impact counseling for her behavioral problems, whereas to correct a lot of the issues with Kelsey and to give myself and her mother a way to communicate properly with our daughter. Right smack dab in the middle of the planning phase, if you will, my ex-wife decides to drop a bomb on me. She couldn't have done the correct thing or the right thing if you will, but rather had to make things much worse in the situation by doing what she did. She knew that Kelsey had a problem with lying, also knew that she had a behavioral problem, also knew that she was hanging around the wrong kids at school, and knew that she made things up, yet she decides to do what is coming up!

This whole ignorant situation launched a CPS investigation on me, and sent Kelsey to a sexual abuse counselor in Kentucky. Given Kelsey's track record for lying, and talking bad to her mother, Leslie should have known better about what Kelsey had told her mom. Lord, I don't know if Leslie drug it out of her, by quizzing her, or if Kelsey had just come right out and told her mother; but the fact that it got twisted into something it clearly wasn't, was an insult to my abilities to father my child. I was not only insulted but flabbergasted that Leslie would do such a thing. It really takes a "special person" to cause intentional conflict that shouldn't have been there to begin with. As if I wasn't under enough stress, having to deal with this was embarrassing to my whole family. It started to become "very clear" to me that Kelsey and Leslie didn't care anything about me as her "father", nor did she care about her mammaw and pappaw in Florida who spent a lot of time with her as well. She didn't care about anything but Kelsey, and the money which they were getting from us. In common terms to express this, what this was in my opinion was pure extortion of money, by gunpoint.

Could you imagine how I felt during this? I felt like I was betrayed and was being put under a microscope for nothing; not one single time did any official ever come to my residence to question me, not 1 single time did I ever get asked about what was going on.

123

I was so darn mad that I could have ripped a tree up by its roots and threw it. This situation threw me into a deep depression, and my blood pressure went through the roof. I had to start seeing a social worker, psychologist, and general practitioner because of my mental state. Because of all of what was going on, I couldn't mentally function in my job. I went from the chipper, happy all of the time guy, to a train wreck of emotion, uncertainty and had a complete lack of motivation to do anything. I was grouchy, and frankly not able to function very well. I couldn't sleep, I couldn't eat, heck I could barely drive my car.

In the mix of all of this, not only was I working a full time job; but I was also an entrepreneur trying to build a business. Myself and several of my other business partners had a convention that we were to attend in Oklahoma City Oklahoma during the weekend, so we packed up our bags and prepared for the trip. One of our more prominent Directors was going to drive, so I had Mary take me over and drop me off at his home office; and we left from there. It was a 12 hour drive from Kentucky, and we all took turns driving; but the Director did most of the driving, since he wanted to. During the course of this, my attorney in Kentucky was dealing with the crap that my ex-wife started. I really wasn't myself during the course of the paperwork, if you will, but he and I worked together, in a very slow process. It was a long, drawn out, expensive venture, and why but for no reason, except to cause me further problems with my daughter. It took from then until sometime in May, and the case was dismissed because of the fact that the complaint was "unfounded". During the course of all of this, my attorney, at my request, filed a court ordered restraining order against Kelsey and my ex-wife, preventing "any" direct contact with Mary, my mother and father, or I. It was during this time, that I lost any confidence or trust in my daughter or ex-wife. For a child, who is the most important person in your life, to turn on you, and stab you square in the back with a knife like this, to say the least, was hurtful, and broke my heart in two.

Not too much later, given any time whatsoever that I had left, I took my "Last Will and Testament" out of my fireproof lockbox and looked it over in mid-July of 2013. It was not my wish, nor my will to have to revise my document, but after what I had dealt with recently with my oldest daughter, I figured it was about time to sit down and give it some good hard long thinking. I read over my Will, and laid it down, drank some coffee, read it over some more, and put it away. A couple of days later, I went and grabbed my copy which I had in one of my filing cabinets, and started with my ink pen, making changes to the document. I made some changes to my executors, my dependents, my beneficiaries, and a lot of other aspects to the document. It needed revised anyhow, but this was just as a good of a time as any, so I went to my desk. At this point, I didn't see any reason, at all, to keep Kelsey as a beneficiary of my estate, nor did I think she deserved anything. I called and spoke with my attorney's office, and they informed me that I had every right to exclude anyone who I wanted to from my Will, including my own child. They also informed me, since I didn't want a fight breaking out at my reading once I passed away, that the Will could not be challenged, because when it was drawn up, notarized, and copied back to the law firm, that I was in my right mind upon the signing of the Will. This means that even if anyone wanted to challenge the Will, they couldn't because I was of sound mind and body when I put my signature on the line in front of a public official with Notary rights. It was at this time that I dis-inherited Kelsey from my Will, because of the damage that she had done within my family. It really takes a lot to upset me, but these actions and me being her father, I was not going to stand by and let her treat me that way; so I took legal action in the form of my Will. I hated to do this, but it was a sure fire way to ensure, nothing in my possession went to her, upon my passing. I was willing, however, to later revoke my decision, if things turned around and she came back to me, sorrowful of her actions, but I wasn't about ready to hold my breath.

Chapter 34 - The Runaway Juvenile Delinquent

It was October 28th 2014, late at night, and I was sitting in my apartment with my wife Mary, and my two beautiful children. I missed my girl, because I hadn't seen her in ages. For me to go from seeing her on a frequent basis, to not seeing her at all, wreaks havoc on a heart. At the time, I had a Facebook account, and I get a long list of messages from a person that I didn't know of before. Now, at first I didn't put two and two together, because all I saw at first was a friends request, but once I dug down into my messages, I saw a girl who sent me a message. I replied back, "Kelsey didn't put you up to messaging me did she", because I knew I had a court ordered restraining order in place that I had my attorney file. After digging a little further, there must have been 20 some messages and 40 pictures.

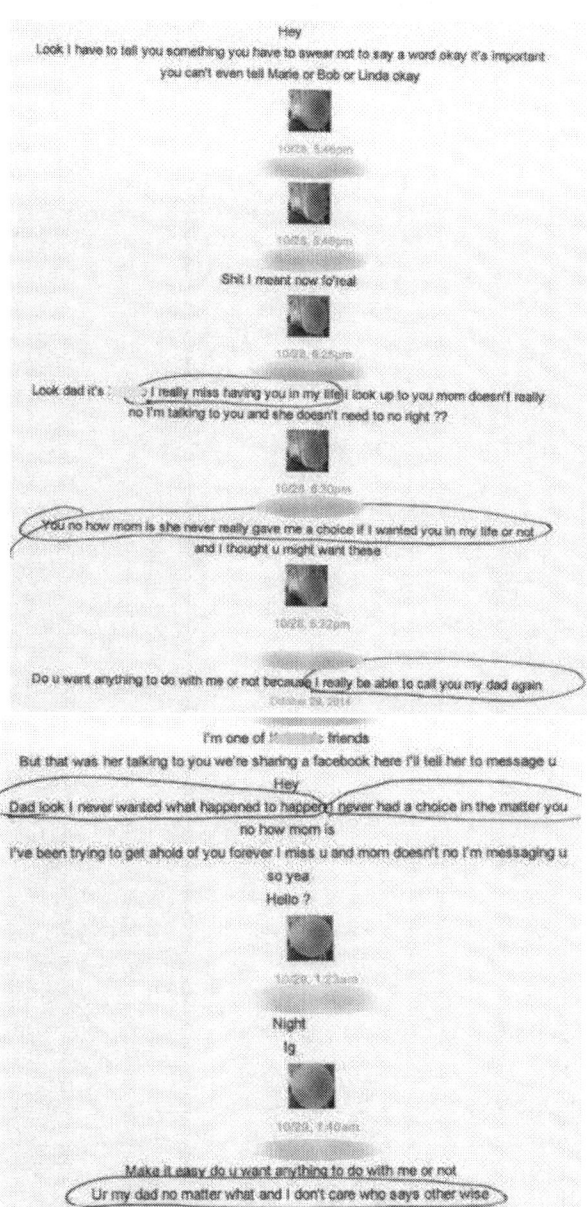

The girl, whom the account belonged to, said that was
Kelsey and they were "sharing" an account. She didn't even give
me time to say that I couldn't speak with Kelsey, but my daughter
told me that it was her mom's fault, and she knew her mother was
keeping me from seeing her, and that she was sorry, and wanted
me to have a bunch of pictures of her, asking me if I wanted
anything to do with her. It was all I could do to not respond, while I
was sitting there in amazement that my daughter would ever contact

me at all. I looked over at Mary, and said, "You will not believe who is messaging me".

I get a call from my father in Florida, who was on just an equal lookout for information about my daughter, as I was. We know the environment my daughter was being raised around, and none of us liked it, not one bit, because we knew that no one was really keeping a close eye out for Kelsey. I told Leslie years earlier that she had better keep a very close eye on Kelsey because I knew, at some point, Kelsey, who was now almost 16 but at the time was 14, was going to start climbing out the window in the middle of the night. Call it a hunch, but when I was a kid, I snuck out in the middle of the night too, and so did most every other kid, except she was a girl, and I didn't want her getting into something that she shouldn't. The very next morning, dad enlightened me, as to the "situation". Apparently, Kelsey and her "friend" whose account she was contacting me, decided to take off in the middle of the night. I talked to her friend, a couple of months later, and she didn't know what Kelsey's plans were, but apparently Kelsey had walked across town, in the middle of the night, not telling anyone where she was going, to meet up with this girl. Of course, I wasn't informed about any of this by state officials, nor the CPS office, nor anyone else, except my father. The next thing I knew, there was a missing person's report put out by the State Police, for 2 missing teens. My ex-wife and her husband didn't have any courtesy, whatsoever, to let me know that my daughter was missing, as if I would press charges on them for informing me about the safety of my daughter. In my opinion, that was just a complete dereliction of duty on the part of their logic and their ethics. How many times do you see these reports on the news? How many times do the teens actually show back up, and how many times do these missing girls end up dead? I was a complete wreck over this. I put a bulletin out on Facebook, to all public, asking about the safety and whereabouts of my daughter. Yes, I know I had a restraining order in place, but there comes a time that the safety of my daughter comes before all "law". There were even postings on just about every news channel on the internet in the areas where she might be. Before 48 hours were up, they found my daughter and her friend safe, and they were at her friend's house in town, but still, something worse could have come of that. I know this information only because it was posted on the internet that they were found.

An entire month passed before someone actually responded to my public Facebook message asking about the safety and whereabouts of my daughter. As luck would have it, a neighbor of my ex-wife, who was "friends" with my daughter, contacted me on Facebook to inform me that Kelsey was home and was safe. It was a relief to hear this, but there was a lot of question in my mind, as to the "real" reason behind contacting me. The neighbor informed me that Kelsey was coming over to her apartment and wanted me to speak with my daughter, and asked me if I would say anything. As much as I would have loved to speak with my daughter, there was a restraining order that I had filed, and they knew it. The neighbor even asked me an "entrapment" question asking how I felt about my daughter. Come on, Really? I don't feel that way about my daughter, and they all know it; but they really wanted me to respond to that? I couldn't believe what I was seeing. She said that I was the topic of conversation when Kelsey came over - I bet I was!

She can be crazy sometimes in a goof way but !   said something about papers and not being able to talk to you

She's coming over in a little if I let you talk to her would u say anything

Well.I think that's her I gtg

One question tho how do u feel about her

11/24, 6:26pm

I don't

Again... I can't comment

If I said one way or the other then I would be wrong..

I called and spoke with the State Police investigator about this situation, and frankly I was pissed off, to say the least. He said that this was the second time, in a 6 month period that he has had to deal with her, and that she ran away just 6 months prior to this event, whereas he found her with an adult having sex, underage mind you, and that her mother called in another report of her running away. Now, if that was me, the police wouldn't be involved, because I would have a GPS unit on her, and security all around my house to alert me if she tried stepping foot out that door without me knowing exactly what she was doing, where she was going and who she was going to be with. Yes, I know, I am overprotective; but what else would you expect from me, seeing as how you have read with me up to this point? Neither her mother, nor her wanted to press charges on the fella, but again, no one bothered to contact me, ask me what my opinions were on the matter at hand, nor was I ever notified of it, before during or after the fact. Are you starting to see the big picture here? That is exactly what I am telling you, not one single person cares about the safety of my daughter, not the court, not CPS, not the police. If it isn't apparent enough, in my opinion neither does her mother. The fact that she wouldn't let me know what was going on with my daughter, in that drastic situation just goes to prove how "interested" she is in the relationship of my daughter and I, and how she wouldn't raise a hand to "inform" me of any such incident.

Around the later part of the year, somewhere in September of 2014, my father called me again to talk to me. It seems like the stew never stops' cooking does it? Dad said to me, "Son, you better grab yourself a chair and sit down." I said, "Dad, what on earth is wrong and what do I need a chair for?" At this point, I was in the kitchen walking around, and honestly, was slightly disturbed at his tone, because I have heard that tone in his voice before, the tone of concern. He told me that my daughter was in some type of accident back in March of 2014, and that she had a severe head injury. My stomach fell through to the floor because it was my daughter, and although I normally remain calm about things, I said what on earth happened. He informed me that he found out, by sources, that she slipped and hit her head on a couch, and it split her head open all the way around to her ear. According to what he found out, it took 72 hours, two hospitals, several brain scans, and 44 stitches inside and out to get her patched up. Dad showed me some pictures of it and i just about got sick at my stomach, because firstly that was my baby girl, and secondly because I couldn't have been there for her. Again, no one ever called me to let me know about my daughter's injury, not the police, nor the hospital, nor my ex-wife. My daughter recovered, but can you imagine the thoughts that were running through my mind about what happened? There was no way, no how that her injury happened on a couch. After some serious conversations with the CPS office, they refused to tell me what really happened to my daughter, and told me that if I wanted to know, I would have to have my attorney's office find out for me.

That, my friends, was a downright violation of my rights as her joint legal biological father. The people at CPS don't care about a father's needs, their rights, their feelings, nor anything else if it is a man who is standing up. It is straight out biased and sexist, and they have uncalled for behavior.

126a

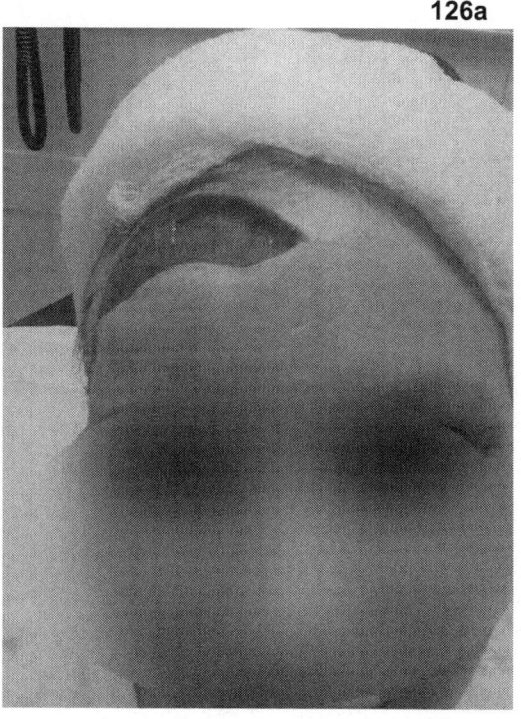

Chapter 35 - The Ship Went Belly Up

Have you heard of the captain who went down with the ship? After the heavy increase in child support, I knew way in advance that it was going to cause me and my family financial hardships, in some way. Before the judge even made his decision, I explained to him that there was no way that I was going to be able to maintain this "level" of support, and that it would damage me. I also explained this to my attorney at the time, and it fell on deaf ears. Neither the judge, nor my attorney had any empathy whatsoever in their viewpoints of how it was going to affect my family, nor did they care. Amazing, that phrase, "did they care." Doesn't that phrase keep coming up in my words throughout the text? There seems to be that general viewpoint in Eastern Kentucky. Honestly, after I left that part of the state, I really learned how much they are still stuck in the 1800's, no jobs, no technology, and for that matter, not much common sense. The outside world doesn't even exist to them, beyond their small borders.

By the time February of 2014 rolled around, I was falling way behind on my mortgage, my utility bills, and my child support. Just like I projected earlier, there was not a chance that I was going to be able to keep up, and this was the effect. What does the world expect? Way more than a person like me could deliver. I started receiving notices from my mortgage company, telling me how far I was behind on my mortgage, and eventually they started sending people out to my house to take pictures of my house, I guess to see if I was still living there. This kept going on for a few months, and frankly I was losing what was left of my mind, trying to keep up. There just simply was no way this was going to work out. The utility companies, water and sewage kept cutting off my services, and the electric company was doing the same. I could barely even keep the utilities on, and frankly it was frustrating and embarrassing. I was doing just fine prior to my ex-wife getting greedy and using me for a paycheck, simply because we had a child together and nothing "at all" had changed with me. I didn't go out and buy expensive items, I didn't buy a new car, nor was I flittering my money. As a matter of fact, I had my money invested in company stock, 401K, and other investments. I was a good manager of the hard earned money that I worked very hard to get, and I feel like I deserved it, because after all of the education, long hours of studying, and various other courses I took over the years.

In April of 2014, everything collapsed that I had worked so hard for. The mortgage company started foreclosure paperwork, and my company terminated my position, because I just couldn't hold myself together. My mental state, my physical condition, and my demeanor changed, and frankly I was grouchy with everyone. Can you even imagine why that was? I was so stressed out, that my hair started going grey, and I am lucky that my hair didn't just all fall out. My kids were suffering because I couldn't provide for them. The child support official in Eastern Kentucky, back in August of 2012, literally said to Mary and I standing in the office, that, "I don't care about your other kids. All I care about is the one you're paying child support on." Her demeanor and her tone nearly set Mary off. Now, if you knew Mary, she is hard to anger, and she rarely flies off the handle unless she gets pushed to that point. It was all she could do to not rip that lady a new rear end, because she was insulting our other two children right to our faces. I will be honest, my blood pressure went up as well, because again, "They didn't care" what they were putting my family through, nor the "damage" that they were causing my other two beautiful and loving children. Exactly what did my son James and Katie do to deserve having everything taken away from them, not a thing? All that the "court" cares about is the first child, and that was stated right out in open court in front of everyone sitting there. They could care less if my other two children had any clothes on their backs or any food in their mouths, as long as "dear Kelsey", had everything and they had nothing. Look, I am not saying that I wasn't willing to negotiate with my ex-wife and the court; to give her what was "fair" to raise her and make sure she was taken care of, but there was a lot of greed going on there.

In June 2014, I was forced, due to no other choice to move back to Tennessee with Mary, James and Katie to be close to her family for emotional and some type of support system. As luck would have it, Mary's sister who lived in the apartments in Tennessee knew the apartment manager and he was able to get us right into the apartment. We had to close out my 401k retirement plan, and sell all of my company stock to live on. I literally had to liquefy my assets to survive. Even with the assets I collected, it only lasted for a short while, because we had to pay rent, utilities, get the children clothes, house supplies, and doctors' appointments for James, because we had to get him back in school. It is never a good idea to move a child from their school, especially when they are younger, and relocate them. It is hard enough for them to adjust to a new school, but they have to make new friends at school, get to know the new teachers and adjust to a new curriculum.

Around August 2014, I had to contact a Bankruptcy attorney's office in Knoxville Tennessee, as I could not keep up with the financial pressure any longer. The process of paperwork took about 2 months, a lot of emails, and a whole lot of phone calls. I had to make several trips back and forth between Eastern Tennessee and Knoxville Tennessee, which kept me quite busy for a long time. The bankruptcy was filed in federal court, just like any other bankruptcy, and took approximately 6 months to complete. By the time February of 2015 came around, the bankruptcy was complete, but that did not make me feel any better about the financial situation, which would not have existed had my ex-wife and daughter put the pressure on me that they had over the course of time.

Chapter 36 - A Mind Is a Terrible Thing to Waste!

There comes a breaking point in everyone's life. That moment in time where your mind could not and cannot handle any more pressure, and you snap. You become someone that you never were. That person is not someone that you like looking at in the mirror, because it isn't you. Imagine if you will for a minute that you went in to get a facelift, and an entire month passes by where you are bandaged up and can't see yourself. The day comes and your doctor takes off the bandages, and you expect a few modifications, but nothing like what you're about to see. You walk over to the bathroom mirror, and gaze into it, and what do you see? You see a completely different person, that doesn't even resemble you. As far as you know in your mind, the face that you have lived with all of your life, is gone, and you have a new identity for all intents and purposes. Of course, your fingerprints are still the same, and most likely your voice is the same, and you know that it's you, but it's not. When you walk out the door, you meet people that you have met hundreds of times before, and say hello, yet they don't know who you are or why you know them. You go to your neighbor's house and say hello, and they don't know who you are either. Some neighbors might think a new neighbor has just moved in and come to say hello, and you know who they are, but they don't know you.

After all that I have been through, I had a complete and utter mental breakdown. Of course, I am getting better, every single day and learning to cope; but the damage that was done to me will last till the day that I die. There have been days that I couldn't get out of bed, due to the dread of what was ahead for that day. I couldn't sleep, I couldn't eat, and I didn't want to talk. Mary has been with me throughout the whole thing, and she can personally testify that I am not the carefree person I was 3 years ago, not even close. I don't know how she has stood to be with me as long as she has, throughout all of the turmoil, but she is a strong woman, duly deserving of a metal. I have, at times, isolated myself even away from her, and talking pretty much was non-existent. I have been to psychologist after psychologist, counselor after counselor, and my general practitioner. I have incurred a lot of time on the couch, talking and trying to resolve, mentally, the problems that I have faced, and I am still dealing with it. Honestly, like I said in the beginning, I feel like I have had a child die, right in front of my eyes, and it hurts me right down to the last cell in my body. My heart has grown cold, and my skin has gotten tough.

When it comes to my children, I am the all-seeing, all knowing eye, which watches over their every move. Call this overprotective if you will, but what I have learned is that I care enough about my children to be preventative. I don't want my kids having skin cancer, so I lather them up in sunblock, I don't want my children falling off of a high place, so I keep them away. I don't want to take the chance in my kids getting hurt. Look, sure there are times that I take my son, who is now old enough, out and let him do things that might be a "little" bit dangerous, like trying new stuff, but he is always under supervision, and the danger rate is minimal by me being there. When I was my sons age, around 8, I remember my dad scared the living daylights out of me; but I know that he sure didn't mean to. That poor man didn't realize what we was getting into before he did it. We lived out in the country, and he was cleaning up a field, just outside of our front yard, to extend our yard, and there was a pile of limbs and stuff and a yellow jacket nest. We both got in his old 70's model Ford pickup, and drove down there. What he wanted to do was shake things up a little bit and play. He hit that yellow jacket nest with the truck, and boy did those yellow jackets get mad. They were swarming around that truck like gnats, and what dad didn't think about was there was a rusted hole in the floorboard of the passenger floorboard. Dad realized that he had made a big mistake and tried to back that truck out, but we got stuck in some mud and the tires spun out. Eventually he got the truck unstuck by rocking it but I knew if I didn't cover that hole up there would be some mad yellow jackets in the cab of the truck. I slid over a piece of wood that dad had in the passenger floorboard and covered it up with my foot. Let me tell you, I was sweating, and I remember it like it was yesterday, but I knew dad didn't "count" on that happening.

After the last 3 years of my life between January 2013 and January 2016, when I am writing this book, I have developed a mental block of a lot of my daughters past. Why? I don't know the real psychological reason for it, although that is what I am in therapy for; but I think it may have something to do with the mental trauma I have been put through, trying to separate myself, so that it doesn't hurt as bad. There are a lot of things that I just can't remember, a lot of things I wish I could remember, and a doubt that I will ever be able to remember them again. I have learned one important thing from therapy however, and that is that I cannot do anything of which I have no control over. In the situation that I have been dealt, I have had no control at all in this. I believe that the psychologist calls it acceptance, but frankly that is a hard pill to swallow.

Chapter 37 - Seriously Misunderstood

Have you just ever just said something that you thought had a clear meaning to the other person you were talking to, but they interpreted it completely different? They look at you with a strange, puzzled look on their face, like they were insulted that you even said that, and here you are with your head cocked to the side trying to figure out why they were insulted? I will be honest, sometimes you just want to reach out and choke the living daylights out of some of these people. I am sure you know exactly what I am talking about. Look, I have never been a person that can portray myself in a correct way a lot, nor am I a person who conveys myself in speech correctly a great many times. I get this strange look from people all of the time, because I might use a word that I think I have a grasp on the "actual" meaning, and my vocabulary gets away from me. Yes, I have used words in my life incorrectly, but then again, haven't we all?

Have you ever done something, in action, that someone else misunderstood? Let me give you a prime example of what I mean here! A really close friend of mine, Sarah, who I went to school with as well, got married back around 2001, and her husband doesn't like me. I guess he feels that way about me, because Sarah and I are so close and she and I talk, but there is nothing there, and I even share with Mary, the conversations and let her speak with Sarah as well. Could you imagine for a minute, and I would actually do this, because she is a good friend, but sending her flowers. I would do this, because she is a nice person, has good ethics, good children, and has worked very hard since I have known her, plus she is an awesome friend. Now, anyone would interpret that as a sign that I was making a move on her, trying to "steal" her from her husband, but contrary to the "perception" that is the farthest from the truth there is. I promote her being married, and I have personally told her husband that if there is anything at all I can do to help them, to call me and I would do what I could do to assist. How is it that a person's actions can be misunderstood? Simple, most people are close-minded, and don't have any perception outside of the "box" than a common housefly. I don't mean it to sound that way, but then again I do because it is the truth. People are on such "guard" with everything that people don't stop to think about the real meaning behind it, or for that matter, just come right out and ask what was meant and take it at face value. Is that their fault or mine? Nope, it's just the way most people are, and a "select" few individuals out there have no hidden meaning at all behind our actions.

Even since my daughter Kelsey has been alive, I have always taken a personal interest in the little thing. I let her hold my finger with her little hand when she was a baby when I would rock her. When she was a little older, I would hold her little hand to make sure she didn't run out in front of a car, or just so I knew where she was. Was there anything wrong with that? I don't think most people would think there was. The older she got, I still held her little hand, because that was habit, and when she was 12 or 13, sometimes, I would still hold her little hand. Why? I don't know, maybe, because I still looked at her as my little 3 year old girl. I loved the little thing, so what would you expect? The only difference, like I said earlier, is others perceptions, right? There was only one major problem. The way my daughter treated me, was like that of a complete piece of trash, a stranger, and talked to me like I was some idiot. I didn't know whether to love her as my daughter, or treat her like a girl I didn't even know. It sure was going in that later direction, because she had changed, a lot, in the way her demeanor used to be toward me.

How do you even, as a father, address this type of stuff? How do you love your daughter and spend time with her, if she "doesn't look at you as her father" anymore, because of what she has been put through, and taken away from her. At this point in my life, I cannot honestly say that I trust her, know her, or even want to be around her; and I hate the whole situation. I have grown to despise the person that she has become. What the heck is wrong with being able to be proud of my daughter, or having a reason to be? What is wrong with being able to talk to my daughter, as an adult, and guiding her, into her adulthood? What is wrong with expecting my daughter to "do good things" and be educated so she will be prepared for her life? What is wrong with her doing what she is told and respecting her father? What is wrong with the whole damn thing? You know, for one time in my life, I would like to be proud of who she is, what she's doing, how well she treats my side of the family, including me, her brother and sister Katie and James, as well as her grandparents. Oh, I can tell you now that I am very disappointed in her, and so is Mary and her grandparents. I couldn't tell you how disgusted I am with who she is and what she has become, as she has become a disgrace to everything my family stands for. I honestly don't think she realizes how trashy she looks now, or how trashy her behavior is, or for that matter, how disgusting her mouth or her attitude has become.

Through my sources, and friends, I have found out some seriously disturbing things about my daughter, which I don't know are true or not, but they come right out of her own mouth, so I am assuming the actions are real. I have had messages sent to me, from other people I know, that she is doing drugs and drinking underage. That she has become promiscuous with every guy she can get her hands on, and seen pictures of her and the way she is now dressing. Yes, I am "really" proud of her. As you can tell, I am being as sarcastic as possible, because I will be darned if my daughter Katie would turn out that way! Exactly where is the good "role model" in her life; her mother and Priscilla, or the husband who can't work because of "medical" problems. As I before stated, he can't work because he has "bad nerves", yet he can do car repossessions with his wife. You already know what that type of person is, and you also most likely know the type. Sure, that is a great example to be setting for your "child", although, I can guarantee you one thing right now. Things would be much more controlled in my house, and that I would pay very close attention to what was going on. For that matter, I have offered on multiple occasions for Kelsey to come live with me, and she wouldn't! Why? Because I have a certain way of doing things, I supervise, I expect a lot from my kids, and she didn't want any "control" over her. She didn't want dad making any decisions, she didn't want me saying no, and she didn't want me to keep her from sneaking out and making an ass out of herself, which is exactly what has occurred living with her mother. Is it a wonder why she is doing the things that she is? Is it a wonder why kids from broken families have these problems? It is because the court doesn't care about the kids, nor do these people at Social Services. Yes, I love my daughter; but there comes a time that a father has to say, "I have had enough", and walk away, which is what has hurt me the most, because she was always my "baby" and now, she is absolutely nothing but a complete stranger to me. I wouldn't even recognize her if I walked by her on the street, and that my friends is very sad!

Chapter 38 - Accountability

At this point in time, on September 28th 2015, I filed a small claims case against my ex-wife for breach of oral and written contract. Now, by the time I am done explaining this, you tell me if there is something going on, as far as corruption in the issues. I will let you be the judge of that, and I will just simply tell you what happened in fact! First off, I didn't need the money, second off it was something for me to do, and lastly, I had never filed a small claims case before, so it was a good learning experience for me in terms of a private civil action. If you know anything about small claims in Kentucky, the maximum you can claim is $1500. I wanted to hold my ex-wife accountable for literally stealing $5000 from me, in terms of the oral and written agreement we had in regards to sending my daughter to the private Christian school in Eastern Kentucky. As I before stated, I don't like liars, and I sure don't like thieving, devious people full of deception in the matter. In my opinion and experience, that is exactly what she did. She needed a newer vehicle, saw an opportunity to get one, took advantage of the situation, entered into an agreement, and didn't follow through with it. Heck, I even lost a couple of hundred dollars back then in having Kelsey's uniforms made. It was all about the benefit of my daughter, and God Almighty himself knows, I wasn't getting anything out of it, except the satisfaction of having my daughter properly educated without interruption.

At the beginning to middle of October of 2015, I filled out the proper paperwork for the case, mailed it to the Circuit Clerk's Office, attached the funding for having the subpoena served on my ex-wife and waited. After a short week or so, after checking, there was a court date issued, as previously mentioned. Attached to the small claims case, was the written and signed agreement (contract) for the Christian school, the cashier's check, of $5000, from my bank which was only 4 days prior to the visit to the Christian school, for the purchase of the vehicle, and a written synopsis of exactly what had happened. I waited the month, for the court date to come around, and then it was about time for the visit.

A friend of ours watched over the kids, in Tennessee, while Mary and I drove up to Kentucky for this "case". We got there, and sat and waited. I wore my best business suit, because I wanted to look professional for the hearing. After quite a while passed, they finally called my case; so I went to the bench to address the judge, and said "Good Morning Your Honor", as to keep with court courtesy. The judge asked me to explain my side of the case, so I did. Now, with that in mind, I had no "idea" whatsoever, that I was going to have to be the one, in open court, to question the defendant. It wasn't in the small claims handbook, as far as I could tell, because I read it. I had understood, the whole time, that it was the judge's responsibility to question the parties involved. I had all of the proper documentation, the timeline - everything. I asked many questions. Now, when it was my ex-wife turn to speak to the judge, she stood right there and lied straight to the judge's face about how many years Kelsey was to be held behind, upon entering the school, and told him 3 years. Now, any moron with a lick of common sense to them would know that "something" was up, if the child would be held 3 years behind. Was this child even getting any education at all? Forget for a moment it was my child, it could have been any child on the planet. The next thing I know, my ex-wife is bringing up the fraudulent "CPS" claim back in January of 2013, which was unfounded, and not to mention the "order" that the judge signed for my own restraining order. Are you kidding me, the judge actually asked the clerk to go get it from the file room, while we waited! Oh, forget him reading my documentation; he didn't even glance at it, to see that there was "factual" proof. Again, he believed the bullcrap that flowed out of my ex-wife's mouth like honey and he was stupid enough to fall for it. Now, I tried to correct the judge politely while I was standing there, because he was getting way off track about the issue at hand, but I was told to in no certain terms, to shut up.

He then dismissed the case, on a lack of "preponderance" of evidence, which was complete bullcrap, because he had all of the evidence on his desk, which was all from a 4 day stretch. That is right, the contract and the purchase of the vehicle, was all done within a 4 day window. I am calling this like I see it; the judge wasn't paying any attention, didn't clearly read my complaint and was frankly sidetracked, so he ruled in favor of my ex-wife. I thought for once, Leslie was going to do the right thing; but it was clear that I was wrong! It became apparent that Leslie wasn't concerned about Kelsey's wellbeing and education. It was clearly apparent however that it was a planned action to get her a vehicle, since I turned her down on the previous car loan. I feel strongly that my ex-wife used Kelsey as a means to get a vehicle since she saw an open opportunity. Upon leaving the bench, on the way out the door mind you, I congratulated my ex-wife, and said, "Well played" in a calm and low tone, and the judge called me right back to the bench. I wasn't loud, because it was a courtroom.

He held me in contempt of court, and sent me back to the jail cell. Mary was stunned, and so was I, because I didn't say that in any tone whatsoever that could have been construed in a bad way. I had to give Mary the keys to my car, because she needed to sit down somewhere. I didn't know what was going on, but here I was sitting in a cold jail cell, full of black mold, in my business suit. I tell you, I was not feeling very well physically, because I was off of my medicine, and didn't have it with me, because it was out in the car, so I was dizzy and felt drunk. If you have ever had to take a serotonin balancer, you would know what I am talking about - it really messes you up if you miss your dosage. When I got to the back, the "deputy jailers" asked for all of my information, and then took all of my pins off of my suit jacket, and took my suit jacket as well. I was being treated like a criminal, and all because of "congratulating" my ex-wife. I asked for a cup of coffee, which wasn't an out of the way request, and they told me no. I asked 5 different times to allow me to call my local attorney's office in Kentucky, and they completely ignored the request. It takes me a lot to get upset, but I tell you one thing, I was pretty pissed off, because I was being ignored asking valid questions. I asked them to go speak with the judge, so that I could formally apologize about any misunderstanding, and they didn't. I also asked them to contact Mary outside and get my prescription medicine, because I couldn't sit or walk a straight line without feeling like I was going to fall over. They completely and utterly violated, and ignored my "civil rights". See, in that part of the county, there is law, and then there is whatever they want to do. I don't think any of the judges, or the paralegals, or even the law enforcement, or officials ever cracked a book in their life. They may have picked their credentials out of a crackerjack box for all I can tell.

There I sat, cold and dizzy, for 4 and a half hours, not being allowed "any" of my civil rights. After all that time that passed, the jailer came and got me, put me in cuffs like I was a criminal, and said that the judge wanted to see me. I had no idea where on earth I was going, or what I was really doing. I had to go sit on convict row, out from front of everyone. Let me tell you, it was embarrassing, and Mary was even floored. After about 15 minutes of sitting there, the judge called for me to come back in front of the bench, and chewed me out for the "incident". He said I was "mocking" my ex-wife, and let me go without any bail demand at all. How many of you would look at this as harassment, and corruption? I have nothing to hide here, go look it up yourself, request the video footage, and you will see that I am not lying or stretching the truth any. It was, amongst everything else that I have had to deal with in that county, a complete and total farce. What I am telling you here is that there is no accountability in that part of the State.

Now, after I managed to finally get out to the car, Mary educated me on what had happened after she walked out to the car previously. There stood my ex-wife, her husband, her sister from Columbus Ohio, her mother, her brother, her husband, mother, younger sister, Kelsey and 2 kids. They were laughing and mocking me, including Kelsey, for trying to hold Leslie accountable for what she did, and the fact that I got thrown in jail because of it. Does that sound like a very good system of "support" to you? For that matter, there Kelsey was laughing at me, right along with everyone else! I don't think that is a proper example to be setting for your child, and neither do a lot of people whom have witnessed it. The whole of their behavior was childish, and uncalled for.

Chapter 39 - The Child Who Hates Her Father

$\mathbf{N}$ot more than 2 weeks after the small claims case was dismissed, around the beginning to middle of October 2015, I get a call from my father again. I learned that my ex-wife, in retaliation, for taking her to court, went back down there again, to the court, to file another domestic violence complaint. It was stated that I was in the neighborhood, where they live, and they had reports that my vehicle was seen. So what, am I not allowed to drive through that part of the state? Heck, I still know plenty of people in that area, and sometimes I do go out there to visit. The domestic violence complaint said that Leslie was "afraid" that I was going to kidnap Kelsey. Oh, for the love of God Almighty! She is my child, and although I would like to see her, I wouldn't hurt or kidnap my child. Heck yes, I have been upset over the years by being alienated, but no one seems to want to take a real interest in helping my daughter salvage her relationship with me. Not one single official, court, school counselors, Social Services, or CPS, has ever made any suggestion whatsoever to have Kelsey and I put into counseling together to hash out the underlying problem. I have suggested this many times, yet it has fell on deaf ears. One would think that my ex-wife would be woman enough to want a resolution between Kelsey and I, her father, yet is this any surprise to you that that hasn't happened? I have even went as far as to write the state representative for the district, as well as the governor's office, but all I ever hear is that it's not their place to handle or help, which is passing the buck. Instead what I am hearing is that they could care less about veterans and their children.

Mary and I were floored, yet again, in the attempts for Leslie, her mother, to keep me from having any control over Kelsey at all. We received this letter from the court saying that I wasn't allowed to get within 500 feet of my daughter, and that I couldn't get within 500 feet of the schools that she "had attended" or is attending at the moment. Really? I called the court complaining about this, because it was nonsense, and they said that anyone can walk into the court and make a complaint and that they didn't have to have any justification, nor any truth to the complaint. For that matter, I was never served process from any deputy, or certified mail of the court date which was coming up, and I had no idea what the real story was that my ex-wife went down there and told these people.

Recently, before all of this I had moved, and the clerk I had spoken with said that it was my "ex-wife's" responsibility to provide my correct address, and that I wouldn't be held accountable for not being at court, if the court date would roll around and I wasn't there. Not more than the time that the court date rolled around, I was expecting, just like she said, that the case would be rescheduled, and they would serve process on me for the new court date, however, that did not happen.

My father called me up again, just following the court date, and my ex-wife was online bragging that she got what she wanted, and that was that I wasn't allowed at all to be around my daughter, who was my prodigy. If it wasn't bad enough that my ex-wife was intentionally ruining my relationship with my kid, she had to go the extra mile. The judge and the court lied about what they were going to do, and they "approved" the domestic violence order until she was 21 years old, so not only have I been without a daughter for 3 years, they are pushing it another 3 years, without letting me even know what was going on by serving me process. I don't think any of the people in that county have a single brain among them, but that is what I have seen and experienced. It isn't fair to the loving fathers out there who really want to be there for the children, and make sure they are properly guided. Although I have two other children at this point, it isn't like I can "forget" that my first daughter was just out there floating around without any foreseeable supervision. Doesn't that just sound like the perfect scenario? Come on everyone that is nonsense!

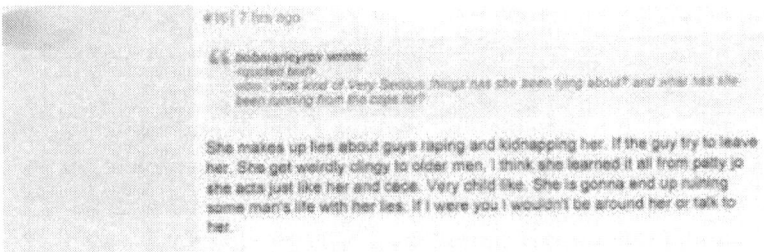

About a month later, I was sitting in my living room, with Mary and the kids, watching Television and trying to relax. I get a knock at the door from the Postal delivery man, with yet another package delivery for me. I signed his signature pad, brought it inside and opened it up. Holy crap let me tell you, this was the sickest, nastiest, stomach curdling, high fetched crap story I have ever seen in my life. Everyone, it was so bad, it took me 2 hours to get through a page, and Mary couldn't finish reading it either, because it was so sick. Due to the "Domestic Violence Order" again re-launched by my ex-wife, they sent my daughter again to the sexual abuse counselor in Kentucky. This time however, she just "happened" to forget to tell them something that was supposed to have happened when she was 12 years old. Oh Come on! Let's all just stop for a minute and think about this. If it really ever happened, they would have reported this back during the first episode that they went into CPS and complained. I couldn't even believe the crap that I was reading, because it was so far-fetched, way off base, and incorrect that even the world's biggest moron could see that it was a lie, yet CPS has the nerve to send this to me? Lord, let me tell you, when I saw that letter, I swear I about passed out, because it was just gross, and it "all" came from my daughter in a meeting with the so-called sexual abuse counselor. This crap never happened, never would happen and never will happen. I have a better chance of believing in Santa Claus at this point in my life than to believe that crap actually happened in my own mental reality. What made it worse, not only was she accusing me of these incidents; but she was also dragging someone else into it that I know in Kentucky. Whoa now! I called this person up to inform him of the situation, and let me tell you, not only was he offended, but he was irate that my daughter would say anything like that about him, considering she used to always want to see him when she would come to visit in Central Kentucky, and she hung on him like she used to hang on me. For the love of God everyone, he is my age!

So let's recap a little here, ok? I was married and had the worst relationship which I could have possibly found. I then was beat down and had a knife pulled on me while I was married to this woman, and had my laptop destroyed. I was cheated on 3 times that I know of and she left me for the last guy, who is now her husband. She has played a game of cat and mouse with my daughter over the course of 18 years using her as leverage to make my life miserable, because she is miserable. She doesn't supervise my daughter, lets her talk to her like she is a dog and my daughter insults me to my face and behind my back, calling me Cleland instead of dad. As time went on, my ex-wife has filed numerous domestic violence orders against me, and has twisted everything I have said or done over time to suit her own agenda. She has turned my daughter into a monster, who sneaks out of the house in the middle of the night, drinks, with possible drug use, and she doesn't know anything about it, and to top it off not only my ex-wife, but now my daughter too is making claims of which hasn't happened.

Chapter 40 - Parental Alienation
...the Worst Kind of Abuse

What we are looking at here is clearly a case of parental alienation; however, all but about 7 states in the United States have abolished that line of laws; so I can't do anything at all. CPS is the biggest waste of anyone's time, the courts are useless; and the law enforcement is just as bad. How do you as a father take care of your kids, when you love them as much as I do? You can't! You are thrown out on your face, denied your parental rights, denied any information about your child, denied everything that makes you that child's father, then she calls you by your name, and calls the other guy dad. Have you ever had something stolen from you like that?

Parental Alienation was a term coined by Richard A. Gardner in the 1980s, to describe a disorder in which a child, on an ongoing basis, belittles and insults one parent without justification; due to a combination of factors, including indoctrination by the other parent and the child's own attempts to denigrate the target parent. According to Gardner, this is a disorder that arises primarily in the context of child custody disputes where one parent deliberately or unconsciously attempts to alienate a child from the other parent. According to Gartner, Parental Alienation Syndrome is characterized by a cluster of eight symptoms that appear in a child. These include a campaign of denigration and hatred against the target parent; weak, absurd, or frivolous rationalizations for this depreciation and hatred; lack of the usual ambivalence about the target parent; strong assertions that the decision to reject the parent is theirs alone, reflexive support of the favored parent in the conflict; lack of guilt over the treatment of the alienated parent; use of borrowed scenarios and phrases from the alienating parent; and the denigration and not just of the targeted parent but also to that parent's extended family and friends.

Cited https://en.wikipedia.org/wiki/Parental_alienation_syndrome

This is a biased scenario by a parent aligning with the child to see the other parent is the enemy. This is seen by the child, whereas they've been convinced to keep the child's' relationship with the alienating parent is to reject the father. Children should not be put into a position where they are being coerced to love one parent and hate the other. In a position such as this, the child needs counseling, love and support in a safe place where the message is that it is okay to love each parent equally. Although it is clear that parental alienation has occurred, the court system in Kentucky does not recognize this. The court has received no factual or proven reason that the father has done anything to affect the health or physical being of the child, yet the fathers being forced into a position where he is not able to be a part of the child's life. It is in this case, that Kelsey's mother thinks that's the way Kelsey is, and that it is natural and normal for her to treat her father or others this way and it is obvious that she supports it.

I don't believe that her behavior is appropriate towards her father or anyone else, let alone any recommendations to reconcile. Not one time since my daughter has been born, let alone in the past several years where there has been obvious alienation, have I one time seen any suggestion whatsoever by Leslie to support counseling to rectify these problems. I couldn't say whether counseling would have worked or not as out of all of the suggestions that I have personally made, it has been completely ignored. I keep hearing, from the court, social services, and my ex-wife that I have done so much to traumatize Kelsey, but it's quite simple that they don't want counseling because they don't want to address the actual problems. My major concern is how am I supposed to foster a normal healthy relationship with my daughter as she moves forward into adulthood.

I agree that there is no way to force my daughter to move her mouth, love her father or go to counseling without coercion from her mother. Because of all of the alienation that has occurred over the years, I don't believe that this is a situation where my daughter should be living with either myself or her mother, but rather in a safe and nurturing environment that fosters love for both parents or at least until the daughter comes to terms with who she really is. It has become clearly obvious, because of the alienation, that my daughter does not know how to love me, and that is a real psychological issue. There has never, not one time, been an opportunity for observation of how we are around one another or how we interact with one another. All that was ever looked at was what her mother "says", so she could sabotage the relationship with her father. I've got to give Leslie credit, because whatever she has done all of these years, she has been successful at it, as she has been on a campaign and has successfully damaged my daughter. It is a real shame, because my daughter does not realize what she is doing. Just like any teenager, they think that they know everything, they think that they have a grasp on reality; and they think that nothing can harm them. That is only where experience, which comes from age, comes into play. The older we get, the more knowledge that we accumulate, and the more chance we have to make sure we do things right. The old saying that hindsight is always 20/20 is true. How many times do you wish that you could go back in time and correct something that you did wrong, but in our technology, at least as it is today, we do not have the option to do that. It is my suggestion for every child, for every parent, for every friend to treat each other with respect, love, admiration, and encouragement, for we do not know when the last breath we are going to take in this world. For all we know, five minutes from now one of us could be deceased. Then what? Is the child, who has been following in the alienating parent's footsteps, going to shed a tear, have regret, or all of a sudden realize that it is now too late to do anything. Once you are gone there is no coming back from that, there is no coming back from time, there is no way that we can rewind the clock and spend time together. What I am trying to say is make the best use of your time, not only as a child where they think that there is no end, and as an adult where we are running short of time.

Throughout time, I have done thorough research into parental alienation and have found the following. You'll find some of my notes attached just below as it is what I have dealt with over the course of the time my daughter has been a child. No parent nor child should ever have to deal with this.

Here is some research I have done on Parental Alienation/Brainwashing of Custodial Parent against Non-Custodial Parent.

1. http://www.nj.com.news/index.ssf/2010/05/nj_appeals_court _allows_lawsui.html
   a. Including false accusations of sexual abuse — where parents could seek monetary damages in civil court.
2. http://www.legalmatch.com/law-library/article/parental-alienation-syndrome.html
   a. On multiple occasions my ex-wife has accused me of being unstable, uncooperative, unwilling, and though I tried to communicate she becomes hostile, argumentative and unreasonable. It's not just me, my parents as well as Mary can attest to this fact.
3. http://family-law.lawyers.com/visitation-rights/Parental-Alienation-Syndrome.html
   a. My daughter got mad at me for badmouthing her mother in front of her. The fact is that I was

explaining to her that, at the time, her mother couldn't afford the things I did for her and she should enjoy them. I also explained to her that she needed to concentrate on her education and that I have tried to get her mother to go back to school however she didn't want to, and that she shouldn't use that example to base her life on. I explained to her that I continue to set goals for myself and that education is extremely important.

    b. I have been told by my ex-wife that Kelsey didn't want to see me, and also my daughter told me she didn't want to see me as well. This was during the Christmas episode. After speaking with my attorney, he advised me that I should attempt to see my daughter even with CPS saying that I can't, since there was no document from the court saying I couldn't, to continue to prove my aspirations to be with my daughter during visitation. I called my ex-wife and politely explained that I would like to see my daughter. This is probably what started the first Domestic Violence Order, as signed by my ex-wife to keep me from seeing Kelsey.

4. Letting the child choose whether to visit with the other parent.

    a. My ex-wife has pulled this on too many occasions. During the times that I wanted to see my daughter. As previously mentioned I would drive 3 hours to see Kelsey and on one occasion called her up to get her to go with me to the planetarium, however Kelsey told me that she didn't want me to pick her up and that she wanted to go to Gerald's dads. I explained to her that I came a long way to see her, and Kelsey didn't care, nor did I get any support from Leslie in doing so.

5. During Christmas, due to all of the conflict, I wanted my daughter to know the reason for me and her mother not being married anymore. I figured she was old enough to understand at this point. I did explain to her a lot of the details. but also told her I made my share of mistakes and her mother made a lot too. I didn't place the blame on either of us. I wasn't upset, but wanted Kelsey to know that none of us are perfect, including me. Kelsey didn't seem to want to talk to me much at all.

6. Not 1 single time in 18 years has my ex-wife brought my daughter half way to see me, expect if I was 30 minutes from their home. I am expected by her to drive the whole way up, the whole way back and the whole way up and back again. In total, where I was living at the time, that was a total of 716 miles every weekend I was to see Kelsey, when it should have been half of the given mileage. I went way out of my way to see my daughter.

7. My ex-wife has told me she didn't feel comfortable with Kelsey coming with me on visitation because she worries about Kelsey being safe with me. Seriously? I have talked with my ex-wife about this on too many occasions about my same exact feelings. How exactly do I know my daughter is safe when she is with my ex-wife? I have always been alienated like I am just some guy around my daughter and not her father. This has bothered me for years.

8. I feel that my ex-wife has encouraged my daughter to have anger towards me, but given everything else you have read, logic would dictate that is the case. My daughter's behavior toward me for the past few years has increasingly got worse, as you can tell.

9. On all too many occasions when communicating with my daughter over the phone, I have caught my ex-wife as well as her husband listening in on the conversations with my daughter. There is no privacy speaking with my daughter at all.

   a. On one occasion I had to call my ex-wife's house to get my daughter on the phone to correct her actions and be a responsible parent. My ex-wife told me she wouldn't let me talk to Kelsey because she didn't want Kelsey to be upset. Leslie accused me of being mad. I told her I wasn't, nor was I raising my voice, but I was being quite firm. My daughter's behavior in minding me was out of line at the time. I asked multiple times for her to put Kelsey on the phone and she wouldn't. This really led to an argument between my ex-wife and I. I do not like to be held back from doing my job as a father, because that just makes me mad, at which point Gerald got on the phone and threatened to break my arm. This has happened multiple times. This happened around October of 2012.

10. As far as unresolved anger towards me, every conversation between my ex-wife and I seems to have her bringing up

when we were married, and what she liked and didn't like. My ex-wife accused me of being a sex addict on the phone while I was in Alexandria VA back in November 2012. I don't know how she can possibly judge that, since we haven't been together in 14 years. I can't believe she still lingers on nonsense that happened in a relationship over 18 years ago. Mary has told me on multiple occasions that she believes that Leslie somehow still thinks that we are still married, and I tend to agree.

11. My ex-wife has stated on multiple occasions that she thinks my daughter either has multiple personality disorder or is bipolar. Either of which is detrimental to my daughter's well-being. As far as I am aware, Leslie has never taken my daughter to get tested, and if she has, I have never been informed. What is strange is that even knowing that, my ex-wife still believes the lies that come out of her mouth.

12. My ex-wife has admitted to me as well as Mary when in discussions with her that she is living life through my daughter. I don't like this, not one bit. This in itself is dangerous to my daughter. There is a difference in raising a kid and being only a friend to your kid. No one can successfully raise a child that way.

13. My daughter used to stay at my ex-wife's mother's, after school, but even Leslie has admitted to me that her mom doesn't watch my daughter. Can you imagine what my daughter can be doing while unsupervised? I sure can, and as you have read, there sure has been a lot of it!

14. While my daughter is in my care at my house, there is never any mention from Kelsey as to what is going on at her mother's. No information is ever volunteered, and normally when I ask her, she doesn't tell me much. On the flip side of the coin, when my daughter goes home to her mother's, I always get phone calls from Leslie mad about something because Kelsey goes home and tells her mother everything and it is usually skewed. and not what was said. Too many arguments have developed over this behavior.

Given the information that I just provided to you, would you or would you not agree that this is parental alienation? It has been quite difficult on my family over the course of these years to put forth the effort in order to spend time with my own child, and as a result of this alienation my own daughter does not want anything to do with me at this point in her life. What you have just read also is nothing but a double standard, one sided and biased upbringing of my child.

Could you imagine being put into a position where as you had to deal with this? There is a lot more than just what I've provided, but I've decided to omit a great deal of it because there would be no end to this book.

In parental alienation, where you are talking bad about one parent that you are insulting and poisoning the child because they are half of you. If this is the case, you are poisoning the child about themselves which is very crucial to understand. One thing that I have never understood, is why my daughter never opened up to me, or talked to me about the things going on at her mother's house. In the past few years I have begun to understand why. It's not like that I could ask her what it was like for her when her mom said things about me. I have had no opportunity to show her any empathy at all, because of the bottleneck in communication

These estranged children, nowadays, have become adult bullies and narcissistic adult children. They threaten that they won't let us speak or talk with them unless we accept guilt for all of their feelings, their bad decisions, and their failures, or unless we except repeated mental torment and beatings. Unless we love them and like them unconditionally no matter how rotten they have been, their manipulation and control will continue to go on and on. We are condemned if we do something good and condemned if we don't. The more we give, the more they torment us, unless they are nice for a while because they want something to their benefit. Over the years I have seen this behavior all too much from both my ex-wife and my daughter.

The bitter truth of the matter is that they have learned this behavior from the alienating parent. We will never say the right things that they will accept. The truth of the matter is that we will never do enough for them. The truth of the matter is that we can never do the right thing, anytime we try, in their perception of us. They will never forgive us and act nice. They just don't have the same values, rules and ethics that we do. I demand quality for myself, my peers, my coworkers, and my children. I would not ask any less of anybody that I would not ask of myself.

Chapter 41 - Hindsight is 20/20

Okay, so what comes first the chicken or the egg? Looking back over time, not only myself, but everyone that I know, everyone that has ever been, realizes that there are things in their life that they wish that they had some control over to change in the past. Would you not agree with that? None of us are perfect, none of us walk on water, and none of us are beyond making mistakes. If we were beyond making mistakes, there would be no learning, there would be no experience, and there would be no certainty. Do I wish that I could go back in time and change some things? Absolutely!

Knowing what I know now, and as protective as I am of my children, the first thing that I would've done, right out of the gate, is to take the court up on their initial observation, when I filed my divorce proceedings, and took custody of my daughter immediately. My daughter to this day does not know what her mother has done to me in the past. I am doing just fine raising my other two children, we play games, we laugh, and we go everywhere together. My younger daughter Katie has become a prodigy for me as well as a project. She looks a whole lot like her older sister, yet she is nothing like her. She is the polar opposite of Kelsey, and at least, I am raising her, I have control over her, and I enjoy being around her. I can teach her what I want to know, educate her the way that she needs to be, teach her ethics, control, and how to treat people. I can teach her to be a professional in her career field.

My son James is quite an intelligent young man. Although he is now eight years old, his aptitude for mathematics is just like mine. He has a significant interest in science and technology, and as amazing as it is, just like any other child his age in today's times; it is natural for him to be able to use a computer and learn. It is amazing how much he is like me. When I look at him, I see myself at his age. I had a learning problem, I was slow in school, and then I had to have tutoring. James is no different, and it is a visual learner the same as I am. All of the advanced mathematics that I have had to learn for my career field, I am teaching him shortcuts in how to do problem equations. He rarely ever shows his work, nor did I when I was in school, yet we get the correct answer. Imagine that! He is still a little young, but he has been asking me for the longest time to show him some chemistry. I am reluctant to do that yet, because his attention span is not tuned to concentrate for long periods of time. By the time he reaches 10 years old, I will have taught him some chemistry as well; but that is a couple of years away yet.

The two children that I have living with me, James and Katie my babies are good kids. What I cannot be certain of is that my daughter Kelsey is a good child. I have learned from multiple sources, and experienced it myself, that my daughter is quite sneaky. It was found that she was sneaking as early as nine years old, at her aunts and uncles house drinking, and that they provided the alcohol to her knowingly and willingly. Somehow, in their mind, it seemed okay for them to do this. What on earth were they thinking? Not only is this illegal, to provide alcohol to a child, but it is also dangerous, irresponsible, and can affect the health of a child. It was also found, as early as 12 years old she was getting drunk with friends of hers, while her mother and her husband were not paying attention, as usual, and Kelsey is out literally chasing a train. Let me ask you a question? What type of person would not be watching over their children, or know for that matter that they were getting drunk? What type of person would not know where their child was, especially if they were outside chasing a train, at 12 years old?

My daughter has run away on three separate occasions, from home, and has had State Police involvement. She has been on the news, and on the internet, and the authorities will not take my daughter away from her mother. In addition to this, my sources tell me that Kelsey has been skipping school at the high school she attended, smoking marijuana and Lord knows what else. Let's use a little bit of common sense. Did I know about any of this as her father at the time? No sir! Had I known about this at the time, I would've gone to the police department to file a formal complaint. For that matter, even if I did, they would leave my daughter with her mother and put her in further danger. My huge question here, is when are the legislators, who govern the laws of the states, going to step up to bat and set some laws in place to protect the fathers' rights, or for that matter set aside all of this nonsense that women, no matter what they do or say, are better at raising kids than fathers? When is enough, enough? This biased nonsense needs to stop. How many of you would agree with that?

Another one of my sources put Kelsey at a no-tell motel in the city limits right on the main stretch of road at 16 years old. I was in town visiting some friends and family one week, and was driving by and realized that the State Police whom I spoke to previously mentioned something about finding Kelsey in one of her run away events in the city area. With all of my previous law enforcement experience, I had a "cop hunch" turned the car around in the road and went right back to the motel. I would say it was somewhere in the neighborhood of 4 AM, and I knocked on the office door of the motel and spoke with the manager on duty. I showed him the 30 pictures that Kelsey had previously sent to me on Facebook on my cellphone and asked if she looked familiar to him. What you know, he said absolutely, and that she checked in sometime in June to July of 2015, but didn't have any identification with her. He let her check in with cash, and put her and the person she was with in the back lot room of the motel. I was irate to be honest about it, because I am her father, not some circus show freak, and I do pay darn close attention to every move my kids make. I told the attendant that it wasn't his fault, and that she took advantage of him being nice, and that was the truth. He asked who I was, and I told him I was her father, that she was 16 years old, to which he responded, "That is illegal". I responded back, and said, "No kidding it is", and informed him that if he ever saw her show backup to notify the authorities immediately. He went on to further explain to me her demeanor when she came in, and that she was inebriated and talking fast. I reported this to CPS, and they drove to her residence and asked Kelsey if she was at the motel to which she told them no. Do these idiots actually expect a teenager to tell them the truth? They dropped that investigation as well, with no further looking into it. I wasn't surprised at that either!

For that matter, it was discovered that my daughter was sneaking out of her mother's apartment through the second story window, to sleep with her boyfriend, in the middle of the night while her mom was either gone or asleep and Gerald playing on the computer.

Yes, I do my homework. As you can tell her mother doesn't watch her very carefully, and if she is allowing it, she is not doing her job if she knows about it. As I previously mentioned, my daughter has become quite devious herself with her lying and sneaking around, and that takes a person as dedicated to watching a child, as I am equipped to handle it. I can't say the same thing about my ex-wife, because it is obvious she hasn't, isn't and won't do the job properly. If I were able to, and it was my call, I would have had my daughter put on lockdown. For that matter as you can tell in addendums, she refers to her step dad who does nothing more than sit around, a dad, and me, well nothing. As you can tell, there was no mention of me at all. That is really a sad situation. She has had every opportunity to have me in her life, and every chance her and her mother get, they avoid me being a part of it.

I've been going to a psychologist, psychiatrist, as well as a general practitioner, and have been put on a multitude of medications in order to deal with the stress, anxiety, depression, and sleeplessness which have sprouted from the continuance of problems. One of my psychologists explicitly told me that I needed to take a vacation, to give my mind time to rest. I thought that this was funny, as I knew a vacation was not going to have any bearing whatsoever on getting rid of the underlying problem. I told her that when I got back from the vacation that the problem was still going to be there, and that even if I were on vacation I was still going to be thinking about all of the issues. The psychologist recommended also meditation, picking up new hobbies, and therapeutic ideas to help me relieve some of the tension, and I have for the most part picked up these new hobbies so it has given me something to do, yet the problem still remains.

My father called me today, to talk about several engineering issues, as he has forgotten a lot of information from where he was put into the hospital, and had a stroke. My father relies on me from time to time to help him remember a lot of the technical information that he used to know at one point in his life. He and I could spend hours upon hours talking about engineering, technical solutions, and new ideas, because it's just something that he and I have in common and he has been a big mentor for me over the years. He has pushed me, held me accountable, and guided me for the greater good. He has made me the man that I am today, as I have technology running through my blood naturally. Do I regret this? Not a chance! Could I have picked another career field to involve myself with? I couldn't imagine that I could have, as it's totally natural for me to be able to logically work on systems. Although I have the aptitude to be a doctor, I would probably be bored with it. That is the reason why I have tried to push my daughter over the years to be more than I am. Every parent wants their child to be more!

In addition to studying technology, I also have an aptitude for science and physics. I spend hours upon hours watching videos, taking notes, and learning about everything. One of the recent videos that I have watched was of planetary creation, and how the planets were formed. I've also watched the lifecycle of planets and how planets end their life. The end result of either a planet, or a star, usually results in a black hole, with an event horizon that does not let light, or anything else escape. If you get remotely close to this event horizon, you will be sucked in, and completely obliterated. This sounds a lot like parental alienation, whereas the child gets too close to the alienating parent, and can't see, run, or escape the event horizon. No matter how hard you try to get away from the black hole, it will rip you to shreds. I find the mysteries of space, quite intriguing, as there is no end to the possibilities.

Is there ever going to be a resolution to be able to sit down with my daughter? Is there ever going to be a time where my daughter is adult enough in her mind to be able to sit down with me again over a cup of coffee and talk? I'm not asking for much here, except to be able to develop an adult relationship with my child. I don't want this tension to proceed. It's bad for my health, and it's bad for hers. There must be a breaking point somewhere, as glass cannot hit the ground without shattering. I only wish the best for my daughter, her health, her mental stability, and to be able to share love with my child and to have that love reciprocated. So I ask you this, is it possible? It is not my daughter's fault that she is in a situation that she is. It is not her fault that she has been brainwashed into believing that I am a bad father, not her dad, and not able to be there for her!

Chapter 42 – Aftermath of the Damage

So here we are, July of 2016, and the fallout of the damage is everywhere. I haven't had any communication with Kelsey in 3 years. It has been terrible, because there hasn't been a day that has went by that I haven't thought about her. Imagine having a child, whom you love and can't speak with because of all of the turmoil that has happened! I can see and speak with my two younger children anytime I want to. Anytime they want to, they can tackle daddy and play. I get to see their smiles, hear their laughs, feel their touch, and cuddle with them, anytime I want to, and why? It is due to the fact that Mary is a good woman, totally interested in the welfare of our children and she wouldn't keep me from my kids, even in the event we might split up, because we have had that conversation. I told her, and she has personally seen me live, the damage of what has been done with Kelsey and she knows that I would give anything on planet earth to be a part of my kids lives. She doesn't talk bad about me to the children, and she encourages them, the same as I do, to call the other respective parent, be a big part of holidays with us and to love equally.

Over the past three weeks, my mother and father received Facebook friends requests from Kelsey, along with 2 of my close friends in Kentucky, Mary and even myself. I had been informed that this was occurring prior to myself receiving the request. I was sitting with Mary and my two younger children at the automotive service shop, and pulled my cellphone out so I could see what time it was, and there was the friends request. To be honest, I didn't think in a million years that I would ever have her send me a request, but apparently I was wrong. What I have to question is her motive in doing so. Why would I even say something like that? Well, it is really simple! As you can tell from the context of the book, the motive has usually revolved around money, or trying to get me criminally charged with something, because they are miserable in their own right. I can appreciate them wanting to be miserable, along with anyone else that wants to live in the same boat, however I prefer to be happy. I prefer to surround myself with, highly educated, successful people of whom I came from.

"So What!, you ask yourself, "Why would it matter that your daughter Kelsey sent you a friends request?" Well, the interesting thing here, is that I was playing around in my Facebook account and ran across a "filtered" message. In Facebook, a message gets filtered and put into a different message box, than your main inbox, if you are not friends with someone, or if Facebook thinks it is spam. Fair enough, you probably understand what I am talking about. So I happened to look in my filtered inbox, and low and behold, here sits a message from my daughters "flavor of the week". I would be more supportive of her if she had the courtesy to ask for my permission, or talk to me about who she wants to date, or at least ask what my viewpoint is on the person, but no, she doesn't do that. Instead, she just does whatever she wants to do. That, and the "flavor of the week", doesn't have enough respect to come to dad and ask, introduce themselves, or nothing. Did I respond to the message? No way! There was no courtesy whatsoever in the message I received, no nothing. These damned kids need to learn some respect for their elders, and that is the plain truth to it.

The message stated something to the effect that "he" was trying to help Kelsey out by letting me know how she was doing, since she wasn't allowed to talk to me because of the Domestic Violence Order that her mother had filed on me in October of 2015. Interesting I thought! Why would she care enough about me to even let me know how she is doing, because she sure hasn't cared in the past! To her, I was nothing but a money bag that she could visit and use for her own amusement and entertainment the course of her childhood until 3 years ago. I asked her about that at one time and of course Kelsey denied that's how she viewed me, but history has proven different to me. What is that saying? Actions speak louder than words, right? The message also said that there would not be any posting of messages to Facebook, and that no one in Kelsey's family would know that I was talking to her boyfriend about her. It also said that the messages would stay between us, and that if I chose to speak then he didn't want to be a part of it anymore, and that he was just trying to help Kelsey out. Does that make any sense, whatsoever, to you? I am done trying to figure out a puzzle of signals and messages coming from Kelsey. It is like trying to follow the stock market, one minute it looks good, then the next, it crashes.

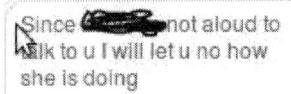

Since ~~████~~ not aloud to
talk to u I will let u no how
she is doing

It stays between us no posts
no other family that's aloud to
no on her side now if u
deside to let that happen I
no longer wanna be apart of
this I'm just trying to help her
out

I am no fool, but that almost sounds like Kelsey wants to get back in touch with her real dad, right? Let's take a closer look at the message and you decide for yourself. First and foremost, why is Kelsey's boyfriend on her account in Facebook. Second, why is he trying to send me a message knowing that there is an order of protection in place, whether true or not, and lastly, after all of the time that has passed, what makes him, or Kelsey, think that I even want to talk to them. Granted, I would love for nothing more than to have a conversation with her, and get back in her life, so we can heal our relationship without the interference of her mother, BUT there is the DVO in place none-the-less. Next, after all of the miscommunication, lies, deception, greed and running to the court every chance they get to file complaints on me, what would make me trust that it would, "stay between myself and whoever" is on the other end of the computer connection. Do you see what I am saying here? How, after all that has happened, could I put myself in a possible position of getting charged again, for something ridiculous, besides, I am a career professional and do not need any problems, along side of what she has already caused.

Later that week, I get a call from my mother, whom received a message on Facebook from Kelsey's Facebook account, asking why her grandmother tried to call her "awhile" back and pretended to be someone else. I had no idea that it really had been my mother trying to verify where Kelsey lived, but she thought she was calling the neighbors house and since my own filed restraining order was in place, she wasn't supposed to be making direct contact with Kelsey either, and that was at my original request, not that I even wanted to have the order in place to begin with. My mother had responded back to this message from my daughter, and found out that it was her boyfriend sending messages on her account. It ended up getting much more interesting in the fact that I am still paying child support in an over-excessive amount. Guess what? Kelsey is no longer living with her mother, the custodial parent, yet her mother is getting enough money in child support that she could drive a Corvette, and I bet my daughter isn't seeing a penny of that money. Why would I think that? It is really simple, because Kelsey had recently made some posts online that stated that she was looking for a job. Why would an 18 year old want or need a job if she was getting that much money in child support? Would you care to ask yourself that question?

During the conversation with Kelsey's boyfriend, my mother inquired where she could send Kelsey's belongings, her drawings and her artwork from where she was younger, since that stuff is hers. Kelsey's boyfriend said that she didn't want to give out any information as to her whereabouts or her address. He said that she is living fine on her own and that she didn't need that stuff after all. He also, when asked by her grandmother, as to why he was on her account, and if they lived together, he stated Yes. Again I ask you, why am I paying child support on a daughter that isn't living at home. Furthermore during the conversation, he stated that Kelsey missed her stepmother, her younger brother and sister and her grandparents, but when asked if she wanted anything to do with her real father, the answer was "I don't think so." That is really sad. It is a terrible way to treat your father and someone that loves her very much. Over the course of time, worrying about her, my health just keeps getting worse. Whether she cares or not is another story, but it is not very kind to treat your parents the way I am being treated by my first child.

A couple of weeks later the messages to my mother continued from Kelsey's boyfriend to my mother. Eventually, my mother had enough of the 3rd party messages and told her boyfriend that if Kelsey wanted to talk to mammaw, then she is going to have to pick up the phone and call her directly, so she would know for sure who she was talking to. Mammaw provided her number to Kelsey's boyfriend in Facebook. Now, no one thought Kelsey would actually call, nor did I. Apparently Kelsey actually called my mother and spoke with her for a long time. Kelsey actually told my mother that she was living with her boyfriend on Plum Fork road, in the county where they are at.

According to the state law, "A parent emancipates their minor child by consenting to the child's marriage. Likewise, if a parent allows a child to move out and become self-supporting, the child is impliedly emancipated." According to the rules of the state, once a child is emancipated, "18 or not", according to child support regulations, then child support stops. Now if my daughter was treating me with dignity and respect, and wanted to be a "part of my family", then I would have had no problems what-so-ever in continuing to pay child support to help her out, however in this case she is not doing what I guided her to do when I was able to rear her, nor is she doing what I would consider to be the right things. As you can tell from the text of the book, she has gone "buck wild" and is running around, shacking up with every boy she can find. If she was doing the right thing, she would either contact me and move to where I am, and let me provide for her, or stay with her mother, which in my opinion is still a bad place to be. At this point, she is living, in a rundown road back in the sticks, instead of having the opportunity of living in a nice house, with a nice bedroom outfit and having the opportunity to let me help her go to college, and finding her an internship with a big company, which I have the capabilities to do. Do you see a problem in her common sense here? She is point blank screwing herself up, because now and later if she comes to me, she is going to be swimming up the creek without a paddle to get her back. In other words, don't bite the hand that feeds you. There are even times in my age that I still rely on my parents to help me out, and if I did what she did, there wouldn't be a chance that they would help me. Get what I am saying?

Due to this, I called and left a message with the child support enforcement person who has been in charge of my daughter's child support, for as long as I can remember, and enlightened her on the topic at hand. I am quite sure that my ex-wife hasn't called to inform her of the change in status of my daughter, because after all of this time, she has been living off of the system and wants every "free" penny she can get from me. Why would my ex-wife voluntarily call and report that our daughter had moved out of her house. There wouldn't be a chance in heck that she would ever do this on her own, because my ex-wife is a deceptive, manipulative, and unethical waste of good air. With that being said, I waited for the child support office to get back in touch with me, so either it can go back to court and have Kelsey emancipated on record, or so she could manually stop child support since Kelsey is no longer living at home, under the care, guidance and protection of her mother, which is the whole purpose of child support. I don't feel that I should have to continue to pay child support to an ungrateful child, or to an ex-wife that flitters money like it's pez candy. What am I telling you? The party train, I am throwing the brakes on, and the money train is coming to a halt. No more freebies, no more are they going to abuse my education, my knowledge and my kindness, in exchange for money that I have no control over. No more am I going to allow this to happen. I am tired of having a money gun held to my head holding me hostage. My ex-wife has abused this for way too long, and has taught Kelsey that it is ok. Well guess what? It is NOT ok, and I have had enough! The whole situation has went from a skirmish, to a full blown war. I am tired of sitting back and taking incoming fire and being powerless to do anything about it. Now… NOW I am breaking out the armament and going to start firing back, so to speak.

Chapter 43 – Last Thoughts

Can you imagine putting yourself in my shoes throughout the course of the contents of the book? It has not only been trying but it has been humiliating, shameful, and shamed my family, my name, and put me into a position where as I have had no control over the rearing of my daughter. I have spent many restless nights sitting up thinking about her and her well-being. For most of you this situation is most likely unimaginable, to be torn between your child and a broken marriage, but has had in the end result of alienation. To have your own child thinking of you as a bad person simply does not make sense in the mind of somebody who cares. I have been told on many of occasion by multiple members of my family as well as the psychologists that eventually my daughter will grow up mentally and see the big picture. Only time will tell if that will be the case, however, given the extreme nature of the alienation that has occurred over the years, I am not so sure if that will happen; but I would like to think that it will. As you can tell from reading, there have been multiple catastrophes over the years; and I'm afraid that this is yielded into a no turn situation.

Up on many of my visits to my psychologists in dealing with the situations, I have been told that there is something called acceptance. This is not to say that I have to approve of the actions of my daughter and my ex-wife, but rather that I should accept and move on for my own mind and body sake. From what I understand, to accept, somehow my mind is supposed to alleviate some of my stress. I'm not so sure that I believe that, but I am an open-minded person to some extent and am willing to try anything that will allow me to rid myself of some of the mental stressors of the situations. At this point I have been seeing a psychologist for around three years, from 2013 till 2016, and I have to tell you it has been three years of the most trying times of my life. Since I have not been able to rear or see my daughter, nor have I had any control over the situation, I have felt helpless and hopeless over any desirable outcome. What I think, what I want, and what is best for my daughter is well beyond the capabilities of deliverance. No matter what I have said, done, or would like to do to help her along the way, there is absolutely no way that it will happen.

Over the years, I have been asked to co-parent by my ex-wife, however any attempt to do so has yielded negative results. The behavior exhibited has been brainless and dangerous and has caused myself and my family hardship over the course of the past three years. It is clear that they have no regard for the consequences of the law and feel that no matter what course of action they take that there is going to be no consequence. Irregardless of whether there's a consequence with myself is another story, but then there is the real world and reality and a lifetime ahead of my daughter. If the behavior exhibited carries forward into adulthood I'm afraid that it's going to lead into major problems for her on the way. As many times as my ex-wife has thrown "child abuse" in my face, by alienating my daughter against me she is the one that is causing child abuse. Just ask any psychologist or social worker, and you will find out that I am telling you the truth, or for that matter spend five minutes on Youtube and you will come to the same conclusion.

Over the years, my daughter has called my father more times throughout the weeks than I could imagine. She never had to find his number, because she had it memorized, and could dial it without a second's hesitation. With me on the other hand, I rarely ever had the pleasure of having my daughter call me to say hello, or see what daddy was doing. I never received any phone calls wishing me a happy birthday, nor merry Christmas, or Happy Easter. On many occasions on her weekend visits, I would write my number down for her on a piece of paper and show it to her, so she could remember my number, yet out of all of the months that went by, she rarely ever picked up the phone to call me up. Additionally, most of the time that she would call me; it was out of a result of her mother wanting something, which is called a pawn. I would answer the phone, and I was really happy to hear Kelsey's voice, only to have her say, "Mom needs to talk to you", and she just hands the phone over. That in terms is known as *"bait and switch"*. Leslie knew that I was upset with her, and instead of her having the nerve to pick up the phone and call me herself, she put our daughter up to doing it for her.

Kelsey and I over the years used to be really close. She used to be a huge "daddy's girl". We used to wrestle, and play, and most of the time we were rough with each other. Have you ever gone down to the creek and had a crawfish pinch you? If you haven't, let me be the first to tell you, it isn't the most pleasant experience that you will ever have. It hurts something fierce. Kelsey was one of the world's worst for biting me. She would grab me and latch on with her teeth, and the only way that I could get her off was to pinch her, grab her leg, or give her a cow bite on her leg with my hand. That girl was ferocious, but I always found it fun to play rough with her, because I didn't want her growing up being a girly girl, and not knowing how to defend herself against danger. Although my other daughter Katie is young still, I play rough with her at her age too intentionally, so she will know how to take care of herself. She is getting to be quite apt at her age already, and I am proud of her for that. My son James and daughter Katie, I have been teaching martial arts to as well, because of just wanting them to know how to defend themselves. I have trained for over 15 years in 4 forms of martial arts, and so I am able to train them properly. I tried to train Kelsey, but I couldn't keep her attention long enough. There was a point that Leslie put Kelsey and her half-brother in a martial arts class, but took them out because of a money issue. I offered to pay for all of Kelsey's training and even offered the instructor to buy their equipment if she would train Kelsey. Leslie wouldn't allow it, because it wasn't "fair" to her son. I hate to break it to you lady, but your son isn't my responsibility. The only responsibility I have is to my daughter, and it wasn't right to keep me from having my daughter trained. Any logical and reasonable person would agree with that.

Since I have been forced away from my daughter by the frivolously made accusations by my ex-wife and daughter, here is a small list of what has happened, and proof of such.

1. My daughter has run away from home on multiple occasions
2. She has been drinking since she was 9 years old. As you can tell from previous readings my daughter admitted to her pappaw that she was in the car with them drinking when she was 8 years old.

me

So how mch vodka cn you handles?

Detroit

Up to five bottles depending on what type mood I am in

That's a day

me

I likez absolute

5 bottles? Bullz

Now whiskey I don't trust myself last time I drunk whiskey I jumped on a moving train my friend actually has a video of me doing it ill get her to give it to ne so I can show u

So a few years back think I was 12 when that happened

...That's why I said grab some moonshine and vadka and hit a dirt road and maybe then we could talk

...rlOh, so how much can you drink, of dat vodka?

...rlI bet dat you couldn't handle a simple wine cooler and you'd be hammered

...3Awe your cute □

...8But sorry took so long I was atthr hospital the horse threw me off □ I'm okay just a concussion

...3Here's my number 270...

Aight' what can you handle den?

...6At the*

...rl98Anything u throw my way □ been like that since I was a little

And its alright

8Oh btw I'm 17 to young for u 18 in June

...girl98And by then gonna be in boot camp □

Your not too yng. I'm 23

What did tha

Tht mean dat anything I can throw at ya. How old ya start drinkin?

Boot camp? For wht? Did you get in troublez?

...Started at 9 and no rotc its a military camp and then after tht gonna go to actual boot camp and train some more and then hopefully get sent off to fight

...3Why u into white girls anyway □ just saying we don't have it all and black girls are so much prettier

You started drinking at 9? Damnz.. where ya get it from? You walk in da gas station n buy it lolz

Military camp? For wht? Never heard of such a thg

...girl98o you've never heard of boot camp ?

Paris island ?

Well that's one of them

...ygirl98No like I said I just grew up drinking all my uncles stuck they stared letting me drink and my aunts plus I snuck out all the time to party

Drunk*

Damz girl, how old was ya sneakin out. Wtf was ya sneaking out 4 if they knew ya was drinking thr stche

heard of it ya, no ideas wht it iz

Lol my mom and dad didn't no I was out or drinking or doing anything else

Haha nvm look it up

Wht? How old was ya sneakin outz the door? What ya mean nethg else. What ya doin lol

8Oh and I didn't give u my number for u not to text meo

My momz would have hung me she caught me sneaking nethg

Oh I wasn't sneaking out the door I went out the 2 story window and took off in my exs truck my dad stayed up late

3. She broke into a high school, but unknown of which one
   - a highschool Spit In a ploices face
   - Okay so I got kidnapped by a trucker and I shot him in the knee Um I drug a girl down a flight of stairs because she kissed my ex by her hair I broke into
     - Today at 8:35 PM
     - me
     - Wtf, why wld ya break into a highschool

   - Today at 8:35 PM

   - Again do u have oovoo
     - Today at 8:35 PM
     - me
     - No, nvr heard of it

   - Today at 8:35 PM

   - And cause me and my friend just woke up and I had the bright idea
     - Today at 8:36 PM
     - me
     - Ya get arrested? Lol for da skool?

   - Today at 8:36 PM

   - no we had hoddies on

4. Hiding drugs for a friend at her high school

- I ment when ya spit in dat cops face

- No skype

- Today at 8:38 PM
-
- That was last year and because he was searching me
- Long story rather not get into it
  - Today at 8:39 PM
  - me
  - God, wtf he searchin for ya yo? Did u put a bomb somewherez lolz

- Today at 8:39 PM
-
- I'm guessing u don't talk to country girls often
  - Today at 8:39 PM
  - me
  - Not many

- Today at 8:40 PM
-
- No drugs my friend gave me to told on to for him because I was gonna take the fall for him
- They probably wasn't real country girls
- o js
  - Today at 8:40 PM
  - me
  - Oh damz, how old wuz your friend lolz

- Today at 8:41 PM
-
- 17at the Time
  - Today at 8:41 PM
  - me
  - I dunno, dey nvr talkd to them mch

  - You do any drugz?

- Today at 8:42 PM
-
- He he didn't exactly give um to me I took them so he wouldn't get into trouble because they was searching lockers

5. Jumping a train drunk when she was 12 years old.

6. Sneaking out the 2 story window of the apartment where her mother and stepfather lives
7. She has become proud of herself, in a bad way

   My names ... im 5'4 Like to travel around love being on the road and im a huge country girl I Love my smart ass mouth I'm a bitch

   Jelaous type Going Into the military Have hazel eyes I'm a dancer I'd rather spend my time bellin hay then at a mall Anything else u wanna no

8. She was kidnapped by a truck driver and shot him in the leg. See bullet point 3.
9. She has been arrested multiple times and has spit in a police officer's face. See bullet point 3.
10. Being   assaulted   by   her   uncle

    * My uncle used to do drugs and he hallucinated and started chocking me

11. Contributing to the delinquency of a minor

Ultimately, Kelsey has been put through a great deal of stress and shouldn't have had to be raised in the environment that she has been, without experienced and controlled supervision. I didn't agree then, nor do I now in how she was raised, and frankly if I would have had it to do over, I would without a seconds hesitation, taken full custody of my daughter from the beginning to raise her, just like I am doing with my daughter Michelle. Trust me, when I say you don't want to deal with what I have gone through, and heed warning to the fact. If you are a parent going through this exact same thing, at least you will have some type of idea of what I have been through and know that you are not alone. I have taken my daughter's upbringing seriously, but have been trumped a lot along the way, because of prejudice and sexist outlooks against men. It has been unneeded and uncalled for, and the people of the court and social services should have been intelligent enough to see through the lies and deceptions smokescreen that my ex-wife has put out there over the years, however, it simply didn't happen, and most of the reason is the perception of "Eastern Kentucky", where it's still an old horse carriage town and a mindset in the 1800's where the *good ol boy* system is still there and quite alive.

There is so much more that I could add into this text, but if I did, there would be a never-ending story that most people could not comprehend, and let's face it, you wouldn't want to read a 1000 page document, right? I would just simply like to say, that I would give anything to just sit down over a cup of coffee with my daughter to talk, but I don't think in a million years that she will. What I think is that she actually believes the nonsense, and with that being said, and as I have before stated, Parental Alienation is a very real and complex topic. For real, have you ever been told something so much that you actually start to believe it, and then it is your reality? She must think that somehow she can avoid me the rest of her life or something! Let's just be frank here. There will come a day that she is going to need my help, my guidance, or something. I have sat and thought about how I am going to react when that day comes that she shows up at my door, and do you know what? I can't be certain that I won't slam the door in her face at this point in my life, but there is also a possibility down the road that I might get over all of what she has done to me. Like I said, if she was sincere and come looking for me with good intentions, then I would definitely sit down and listen, but she reminds me of an ant. When it starts getting a little wet outside, she burrows down in the ground as far as she can get, so she doesn't get washed away. Life isn't like that, you have to stand and fight!

Made in the USA
Lexington, KY
10 June 2018